of the Craft
and
Holy Royal Arch
Rituals of Freemasonry

Brigadier A. C. F. Jackson
CVO CBE

Past Grand Sword Bearer, United Grand
Lodge of England

Past Master, Quatuor Coronati Lodge No
2076 London

Prestonian Lecturer for 1976

Lewis Masonic

First published 1992
This impression 2008

ISBN 978 0 85318 306 8

Published by Lewis Masonic

an imprint of Ian Allan Publishing Ltd, Hersham,
Surrey KT12 4RG.
Printed in England.

Visit the Lewis Masonic web site at: www.lewismasonic.com

British Library Cataloguing in Publication Data
Jackson, A. C. F.
Glossary of the Craft and Royal Arch Rituals of Freemasonry
I. Title
366
ISBS 978 0 85318 306 8

By the same author:

Rose Croix. The History of the Ancient and Accepted Rite for England and Wales

English Masonic Exposures 1760-1769

Scriptural References to the Rose Croix Ritual

Prestonian Lecture for 1976: Preston's England. The Everyday Life of Masons of the Late 18th Century

A Commentary on the Rose Croix Ritual

CONTENTS

PREFACE

When we Masons use the rituals of Freemasonry we are inclined to forget that we are not using modern English but the language written and spoken at least two hundred years ago. It is the language of Queen Anne and the Georges, not that of Queen Elizabeth II. Many of the words and phrases in the rituals when they were first promulgated have, by now, acquired a different meaning, become archaic or gone out of use completely. An additional point of interest is that that the rituals of the Craft and of the Royal Arch differ noticeably in their style and working. The earlier Craft ritual is more direct in style and uses words derived from the Anglo-Saxon language. The later Royal Arch ritual tends to being diffusive and draws much on the many-syllabled words of the Romance languages based on Greek and Latin. The object of this Glossary is to give the modern interpretation to all the words that have, through the centuries, acquired a special meaning or disappeared completely. In addition, without getting too involved in philology, I have tried to show how these words have come into the English language. To complete the Glossary, I have included short biographies of biblical characters mentioned in the rituals.

A. C. F. J.,
Jersey 1992

INTRODUCTION

The vocabulary of modern English is approximately half of Germanic origin, that is Old English and Scandinavian, and half Italic or Romance, that is French or Latin; the latter often being based on Greek. There have naturally been many importations of words from other languages as well.

The languages spoken in England originated with the settlement of Jutes, Angles and Saxons in the 5th and 6th centuries, but the arrival of St Augustine and his followers introduced a form of Low Latin to the educated classes. The Scandinavian invaders, who settled in England during the 10th and 11th centuries, brought many Norse words into the language. Subsequently, with the Norman conquest of 1066 came French, based on Latin and Greek. There were thus, during the 12th to 14th centuries, two sorts of tongues spoken — a type of Latin/French by the upper classes and various English dialects by the rest of the population.

English began to become the main method of speech with the Statute of Pleadings which ordered, in 1362, that court proceedings had to be in that language. The trend continued with the loss by the English Crown of its French possessions and was hastened by Caxton's printing in 1476, the Renaissance of the 16th century and the King James' Authorised Version of the Bible in 1611. During this period many words came from the Low Countries, such as Flemish, Dutch and Low German. The result was Middle English and its gradual development into the modern English which we use today.

This short Glossary is confined to some of the words in the Craft and Royal Arch rituals used by the United Grand Lodge and Grand Chapter, though many of the words also appear in the rituals of other English-speaking masonic bodies. As the development of English Craft and Royal Arch ritual virtually stopped soon after the Union of 1813, the language used is some 200 years out of date. The words chosen in this glossary are those that consequently are archaic, have gone out of fashion, have an interesting derivation or have developed a specialized masonic meaning. In order to complete the story, there are included short biographies of the Biblical characters named in the ritual, together with a chronological table of the actual events covered by the period of the traditional Royal Arch degree.

The Craft ritual used by the majority of the lodges of the United Grand Lodge is that arranged by the Lodge of Reconciliation formed for that purpose in 1813. The material available for the Lodge to use was wording developed over the centuries but principally after about 1700.

It is now possible to date, with reasonable accuracy, the first appearance in masonry of many of the words and phrases in this material from exposures of masonry, masonic books and manuscripts; written before 1775. After this date, by which time there were two Grand Lodges and several hundred private lodges, the multiplicity of sources makes such dating impossible. There is also no doubt that some words and phrases in the 1813 ritual were produced by the Lodge of Reconciliation itself. As a result, the reader must assume that any word, whose source is not given, has not been found in masonic literature until the Union of the period immediately preceding it. An exception can be made for William Preston's lectures which started about 1775 and had various editions until about 1830. Any word that appears in Preston's work may be considered as pre-Union, though it is also possible that it may have been a later amendment.

Words used in the Craft Installation ceremony are included in the Glossary. This ceremony was completed by a Board of Installed Masters in 1817/28 but the remarks above may generally be accepted as applying. However, it is suggested that the Installation ceremony begins to show the influence of a later, less sharp style than that used in the earlier degree ceremonies.

The Royal Arch is more difficult to classify as there exists very little material earlier than the 19th century. Nevertheless one can assume that some material did exist and was examined by the body that decided on the Royal Arch ritual about 1835, but the result shows that the style of the Victorian era was emerging. It was the start of literature with long sentences and words of many syllables. The latter are most noticeable in the ritual, particularly in the lectures given by the Principals which are probably completely 1835 material. Many of these long words, though still appearing in dictionaries, are out of fashion and forgotten. As an example of this trend, the meaning of the word 'monitorial' was a question in a recent television quiz and none of the men questioned was able to give the meaning.

The object of this Glossary is not to criticise the usage of uncommon or out-of-date words but to explain them and thus to make understandable the rituals that we all know and appreciate as part of our masonic heritage.

NOTES ON LANGUAGES AND ABBREVIATIONS

The languages involved may be divided approximately as follows, with the abbreviations used for them in the text:

AS	Anglo-Saxon. Used in England before and after the 5th century.
OE	Old English. Up to about 1066.
ME	Middle English. From *c* 1066 to *c* 1500-1600.
Gk	Greek, usually classical.
C Lat	Classical Latin. Probably BC and before.
L Lat	Used up to about the time of the Christian Fathers, *c* 200-500 AD.
Low Lat	Medieval. Used 6th and 16th centuries.
Lat	15th and 16th centuries.
HG	High German or modern German.
OHG	Old High German.
LG	Low German *ie* Frisian, Dutch, Flemish dialects *etc*.

OF	Old French, from *c* 850 to 1500-1600.
F	Modern French from about 1600.
Rom	Romance languages derived from Latin and Italian, possibly from Greek.

Other abbreviations used:

v	Verb, or when referring to the Bible, verse or verses.
pp	Past participle.
Exp	Masonic exposures (or a specific example). See Note 2 below.
YFR	The Inventory of Mason's Tools in the *York Fabric Rolls,* 1399.
MD	The masonic exposure, *Masonry Dissected,* 1730.
TDK	The masonic exposure, *Three Distinct Knocks*, 1760.
Preston	Preston's Lectures, 1775-1830. (See *AQC* 82, 83, 85.)
Mackey	Mackey's *Encyclopaedia*, 1845.
FGC	*Freemasons' Guide and Compendium*, 1966 B. E. Jones.

HC	Harry Carr, *The Freemason at Work*, 1977.
AQC	*Ars Quatuor Coronatorum.* Transactions of the Quatuor Coronati Lodge No 2076.
OED	*Oxford English Dictionary.*
RA	Royal Arch.

Notes:
1. The figures after the abbreviations of manuscript or book titles in the text are page numbers; except for those following *AQC* which refer to the volume.
2. Most Craft Masonic Exposures may be found in the three following books: *Early Masonic Catechisms,* 1963 Edited by Knoop, Jones and Hamer. *The Early French Exposures,* 1971 Edited by Harry Carr. *English Masonic Exposures, 1760-1769* 1986 A. C. F. Jackson. Books on the early Royal Arch rituals are not sufficiently reliable to warrant quoting.

PART I

Glossary of the Craft Ritual

acacia, an aromatic shrub. The botanical name, according to the *OED,* is derived from the Gk *aké*, (meaning thorny). W. Hutchinson in *The Spirit of Masonry*, quoting Dr Johnson's *Dictionary*, gives *akakia*, (innocence). The original shrub in masonic literature was Cassia (Gk *kasia* or Hebrew *qetsuah*). *Cassia lignea*, cultivated in the East, possessed a fragrant aromatic quality and was used as a perfume at Roman funerals. It appears in Psalms 45 v 8 and as an ingredient of a holy annointing oil in Exodus 30 v 24. Cassia appears first in 1730 in MD and Anderson's Constitutions, 1738. French Exps of *c* 1740 substituted 'acacia', possibly as a mistranslation. Acacia has no Biblical references though it is probably *shittim* wood. No shrub is mentioned in the English Exps of 1760-69 but Preston uses both words. The English adoption of acacia for cassia seems to have been decided by the Lodge of Promulgation, 1813. See also AQC 94, p 203.

Adoniram, under the name of Adoram, he collected taxes for King David (2 Samuel 20 v 24). Later as Adoniram, he was in charge of the levy working for King Solomon in Lebanon (1 Kings 5 v 14). Finally, as Adoram, while collecting taxes for King Rehobotham, King Solomon's successor, he is stoned to death (1 Kings 12 v 18). In the Craft installation he appears as Solomon's architect. The suggestion that he might have been the prototype of the main character in the Third Degree legend is discussed in AQC 5, p 138 and FGC 310-312. The Hebrew meaning of Adoniram is 'My God is Exalted'.

allegory, 'is a description of a subject under the guise of some other subject suggesting a resemblance'. (Mackey) The description is usually in narrative form. An early masonic mention of the word is in *Candid Disquisitions* 1769, by Wellins

Calcott. From Gk *allos* (other) + *agoria* (to speak) became *allegoria* (speaking otherwise). Lat *allegoria*, through OF to ME.

Almoner, the official distributor of alms to others. Since 1910, an officer in an English lodge. Since the appointment of lodge Charity Stewards, the Almoner is now chiefly responsible for welfare. Most other obediences have similar officers but not in the USA where the duties are normally carried out by committees. From Gk *eléos* (pity) to L Lat *almosinarius*, the OE word was *aelmosse* but the present word probably came into ME from OF *aumoner* (F *aumonier*).

apprentice, operative masons usually called those starting the trade 'learners' until the 15th century. Gentlefolk studying architecture, rather than beginners in the mason trade, are called apprentices in the *Regius Ms* of 1390. Apprentices were not members of lodges until about 1650. In early literature the word was often 'prentice' as the dropping of the 'a' before a consonant (aphaeresis) was common in ME. The term 'entered apprentice' comes from Scottish masonry. HC p 10 etc also refers. The word comes from Lat *ad* (to) + *prehendere* (to hold) to *apprentivium* (one controlled). Similar words exist in most Rom languages, eg OF *apprentis* which came into ME about 1350 as *apprentys* (a beginner or learner).

approbation, confirmation or the action of proving something true. The 1723 *Constitutions* conclude with 'a solemn approbation' by the Duke of Wharton as Grand Master. The word also appears in Preston. From Lat *ad* (to) + *probus* (good) to form *approbare* (to assent to or to approve) OF *approver* (F *approuver*) to ME *c* 1700.

apron, appear in the Authorised Version of the Bible (Genesis 3 v 7) as clothing for Adam and Eve. They have been worn as a protection for workmen from the earliest days; and also as a badge of distinction. There are many references to operative masons wearing aprons but the first speculative references seems to be in the Exp *A Mason's Examination*, 1723. Another early reference is in the *Enter'd Apprentice's Song*. After the MD entry of 1730 ordering '15 Fellow-Craft with white aprons and gloves to attend the funeral', the word appears in most rituals. See FGC 449-60. From Lat *nappa* (sheet or cloth) and OF *napperon* (F *nappe* is a cover, table-cloth etc) About the 15th century, an 'a' or 'an' was often joined to a noun, and apron is a misdivision of the ME word 'napron' 'a napron of worsted' about 1560, though Shakespeare uses 'apron' in *Julius Caesar*.

architect, it is not possible to date the first use of phrase GAOTU but its place in the first lines of the *1723 Constitutions* assures its permanency for all Free-masons. From Gk *archi* (chief) + *tekton* (builder) formed *architekton* Lat *architectus*.

artificer, the English meaning is one who makes something by skill, though F has developed the word into a trick or scheme sense. In English, there are no pejorative implications. From Lat *ars* (art) + *facere* (to make). Lat *artificarus* to OF and ME artificer.

ashlar (or asher, astler, ester, esler), a dressed stone block, so called as resembling a plank. Masonic ashlers are either rough or smooth *ie* perfect. In early Exps the perfect ashlar was something called a 'broached thurnel'; the origin of this word being in dispute. A 'perpend ashlar' is a double ashlar used as a binding stone. The word first appears in the *Edinburgh Register House Ms* of 1696 as a 'perpend ester'. Ashlars are in many masonic documents, often as 'a jewel of the lodge'. From Lat

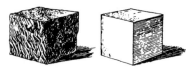

Rough and perfect ashlars.

axilla, the diminutive of *axis* or *assis* (board or plank). OF *aisselier,* OE as(s)heler.

avocation, the word originally (*c* 1500) meant in French a distraction. In ME it developed during the 17th century into any kind of calling or employment. The stem of the Lat verb *avocare* from *ab* (from) + *vocare* (to call) is the derivation.

badge, any form of ornament which denotes rank or office. The Freemason's badge is his apron and is so described in TDK 1760. Etymology is unknown. The OF *bage* has no F equivalent. In ME, it is found as *bagia, bajjie* or *bagy.*

balm, a fragrant salve or ointment made from the resinous discharge from various oriental trees or shrubs. The best known were those growing near Gilead. (Jeremiah 8 v 22) 'Is there no balm in Gilead'? The word appears once in the installation address to the brethren. The salve is referred to by Ovid as used in embalming the dead. From Gk *Balsomon* to Lat *Balsamum*. To ME through OF.

baneful, means life destroying. Bane can be found in expressions as 'He is the bane of my life' or in plant names as 'henbane' or 'wolf's bane (now valerian). From OE *bana* and similar old Germanic words meaning poison.

bark, (or barque), a three-masted vessel, square-rigged, except for the mizzen mast which is fore and aft rigged. The word is used symbolically in the additional explanation of the Working Tools of the Second degree. From L Lat *Barca, barga* to OF *Barque* to ME.

benevolence, means a disposition to do good or a charitable feeling. It was used by Chaucer as early as 1340-1400. The Masonic Fund of Benevolence was started in 1727. The word appears in masonic books, such as *Candid Disquisitions*, 1769, by Wellins Calcott, but not in the ritual until the Union. In Preston, it is stated to be a requirement for a MM. From Lat *bene* (well) + volen(t-s), the participle of *volo* (I wish).

bounds, a landmark or boundary. The etymology is unknown. The Middle Lat is *butina*, *bodina*, OF *bodne*, *bonde* to ME *bonde*, developing into its present form in the 16th century.

brass, the Biblical word '*nechosheth*' is improperly translated as brass. In most references in the Old Testament the correct translation would be copper, though sometimes bronze, a compound of copper and tin. Usually a simple metal would be intended, as in Deuteronomy 8 v 9 'brass is dug from the ground.' The Temple ornaments were therefore probably copper. From AS *Brais*.

brother, the *Regius Poem*, 1390, directs that masons should call each other 'neither subject or servant' but 'my dear brother'. From AS *brothor*.

candidate, the word appears in Payne's Regulations, 1720, to describe one who wishes to become a Freemason; but was probably used earlier. It is not a universal masonic term as other obediences have their own titles, *eg* F *profane* for an initiate and *récipiendaire* for other degrees. From Lat *candidus* (white) giving *candidatus* as aspirants for office in Rome who wore the *toga candida* (white robe) to show their innocence. Candid, as in 'Meek and candid behaviour' has a similar etymology.

canopy, a covering suspended over a throne, shrine or bed. In MD 1730 as 'A clouded Canopy of divers Colours (or the Clouds). From the Gk *Konopeton*, a bed with curtains. To ME through Rom.

chapiter, the top of a PILLAR and is mainly an architectural term. The pillars of the Temple were adorned with chapiters. (1 Kings 7 v 16/20 and 2 Chronicles 4 v 12/13). Though the pillars appear

*Chapiters of the Ionic, Doric and Corinthian Orders
denoting Wisdom, Strength and Beauty.*

in early masonic documents the first mention of chapiters seems to be in MD 1730. From Lat *capitulum*, the diminutive of *caput* (head), the basis for many such words as chapter, capital, *etc*. OF *chapitre* to ME *chapilte*. See also PILLARS.

charge, an instruction detailing duties. Used masonically, the word dates from the operative period. Some 130 Mss, starting with the *Regius Ms* of 1390, known as the *Old Charges*, exist. Charges to individuals, in the present rituals, date from the consecration of a new lodge in the 1723 and 1738 *Constitutions*. From Lat *carricare* (to lay a burden upon) from *carrus* (a four-wheeled cart), to OF *charger* (to burden, load etc). This, dating from the F Exps of *c* 1745, is the source of the English 'to charge' your glasses for a toast.

charity, the primary meaning is 'a disposition to judge hopefully of mankind and to make allowances for its short-comings'. The almsgiving element appears in ME only in the 17th century. The Gk word in 1 Corinthians 13 is *agapé* which implies more nearly 'love'. The Authorized Version translates this as 'charity' but later versions return to the word 'love'. Charity is from Lat *carus* (dear) giving the noun *caritas.* In all Rom languages, it is as OF *chiarté* Anglo-Fr *cherté.*

charter, means a written grant of rights. Appears in Freemasonry after 1717 in conjunction with warrant, but implies continuing power while warrant covers a specific act. From Gk *chartes*, (a leaf of papyrus or palm). The Lat *chartula* is the diminutive of *charta*, to OE *charta* as in Magna Charta.

chisel, a time immemorial cutting tool (Jeremiah 10 v 3 in older translations of the Bible). Listed as a mason's tool in YFR 1399. The word is used as a 'lodge light' in some 1724/25 Exps but disappears for 60 years until it reappears in Preston about 1792 in the ceremony of Installation, and in the 1813 ritual. In the USA it is a tool in the Mark degree; in France, in the Second Degree. From Lat *cisaellium* (something that cuts) with verb *caedare* (to cut). Through OF *cisel* (Modern·F *ciseau*) to ME *chizzel* or *chisel*. See HC 184.

companion, in the Royal Arch degree the companion is an important word. It also describes, in the Third Degree, those standing round the grave. Late versions of Preston also use the word. Mackey suggests that a companion is a closer relationship than a brother. 'All men are our brothers, but not all are our companions.' From Lat *cum* (with) + *panis* (bread) *ie* shares bread with. The word probably came into ME through OF *compaignon*. In modern French masonry, a companion is a Second Degree mason.

compass, a time immemorial tool, appearing in OE in Chaucer (1340-1400) *etc.* The word is in many early masonic documents and the tool was used in some 1700-1730 Exps by the candidate taking his obligation. The word was originally singular, but its use in the plural later was due to the omission of 'a pair of'. The compasses first appear *on* the VSL in TDK 1760. From Lat *cum* (with) + *passus* (step or pace) gives the verb *compassare* (to pace around or measure).

concord, in music, concord is a harmony of notes giving pleasure, as opposed to discord. As such it is in the address to the organist. From Lat *cum* (with) + *cor* (heart) into OF as *concorde* (with one mind) to ME an agreement.

conduces, to help or lead towards a result. From Lat *cum* (with or together) + *duco* (I lead). Through to OF to ME.

convention, means the action of coming together, hence a meeting. From Lat *cum* (with) + *venire* (to come) produces *conventio* (a meeting) and in OF *convention* to ME.

cowan, referred to in the Scottish *Schaw Statutes,* 1598. The first English ritual appearance is in the Exp *A Mason's Confession,* 1727 and in MD 1730 as 'cowan or listener'. The first regular mention is in the *Constitutions* of 1738. According to the OED, the etymology is unknown but it is fully discussed in FGC 421 *et seq.* It is certainly a Scottish word, possibly meaning a dry-wall builder, and so an unqualified mason. See also HC 86-88.

craft (s-man), a common word in ME which developed into skill or art. It is used in the *Regius Ms* 1390, primarily about geometry and appears often in the *Old Charges.* The word has developed into meaning the whole body of masonry. From OE possibly AS *craeft* and OHG *kracht,* meaning power or strength.

cubit, the measurement from bend of elbow to fingertips. There were at least two types, the 'common' or Hebrew of 17½ inches and the 'sacred' or Royal of 20½ inches. The Temple measurements are believed to be the former, but for further reading see *AQC* 102. The etymology of the Latin word is *cubitus* (elbow) based on the verb *cubo* (I bend).

custom, means usage, a habitual or normal practice. In MD 1730, Hiram's 'usual custom' was to survey the work but this changed in TDK 1760 to the current 'return from mid-day prayer'. From Lat *cum* (with) + *suescare* (become used to) giving *consuetudo* to OF *custume* (F *coutume*) to ME.

deacon, the deacon was the doorkeeper of the early Christian Church. In Scotland, he was a higher official, often the master of a trade corporation or guild. The first known masonic usage is in the *Schaw Statutes,* 1599. Deacons were also floor officers or masters of Scottish lodges from before 1700 and, in some English lodges, soon after 1730. The deacon has been an obligatory officer of English lodges since about 1810. See HC 91/3. From Gk *diakonos* and (L Lat) *diaconus* (servant or messenger). OE *diacon*.

degree, it means a stage in descending or ascending in rank or scale. The word first appears in MD 1730 as a masonic degree and has been used in English-speaking obediences ever since. Craft masonry has only three degrees but some other rites have as many as ninety-nine. From Lat *de* (down) + *gradus* (step). The Rom word *degradus* becomes OF *degre* to ME *degree* or *degre*.

dormer, a dormer was originally a window in a sleeping place (dormitory). A dormer-window is a vertical surface, projecting from a sloping roof and is quite common in 'cottage' architecture. The dormer appeared as a 'master jewel' in MD 1730. It is now an ornament of the

MM Lodge and, as such, is in Preston.
From Lat *dormire* (to sleep) OF *dormeor*;
(modern F *dormir*).

dove, doves and pigeons, belonging to
the family, *columbidae*, are plentiful in
the Middle East, and are mentioned
often in the Bible, particularly the Tur-
tle-dove. The dove became a symbol of
a messenger because of its use by Noah
to find out if the Flood had subsided
(Genesis v 8-12). Since 1813, the jewel
of the deacons in a lodge. See also
OLIVE. The word dove comes from the
AS *dufe*.

due, there are two meanings based on the
same etymology: (a) Such as ought to be,
rightful, necessary, the last appropriate to
form the phrase 'due guard' used in many
lodges. See TDK 1760. (b) That which is
owing, as in 'has had his due'. HC 12-3 &
212-3. The word is based on the past participle of the Lat verb *debere* (to owe) giving OF *deu* (modern F *dû*, feminine *due*)
to ME *deu*, *di(e)*.

ebb and flow, modern English usage is reserved for tides. The expression, forming part of an old penalty, appears as 'within the tide flood mark' in the *Edinburgh Register House Ms* of 1696 but, in the *Wilkinson Ms* 1727, this has become as 'tide ebbs and flows'. Both words are probably of AS origin *ie ebbian* (to empty) and *flowan, flod* (to fill). Scandinavian, but not Rom languages, have similar words.

emblem (-atic), a drawing, figure, sign or badge, often implying a moral tale or allegory. The word is used in *The Spirit of Freemasonry,* 1775, p. 109 by William Hutchinson. Early writers appear to have considered an emblem as more visible and concrete than a SYMBOL. This distinction seems to by dying out in modern idiom. From Gk *emblema* (throw in or insert in) through Lat to OF *embleme* to ME.

enliven, to make lively, stimulate, give life to. *En* is the AS prefix to form a verb + AS *lifian* (life).

entrust, means to invest with a trust and masonically implies the communication of masonic secrets or confidential information. Preston uses the word when handing the minutes of a lodge to the secretary at an installation, and for the new master to be 'installed and entrusted'. Of AS or Norse origin. *En* is the prefix to form a verb + Norse *transt, traust* to OE *trust, trost* to ME as *trust* in or *entrust c* 13th century.

equinox, the time when the sun crosses the Equator when day and night are equal. As 'Equinoxall' in *Graham Ms*, 1725. From Lat *aequus* (equal) + *Nox* (night), through OF *equinoxe* (F *équinoxe*) to ME.

equivocation, it originally meant a word that had two meanings but, by the 17th century, implied ambiguity or double meaning, Masonically, it suggests giving words a hidden meaning or significance, other than that they normally bear. The word appears first in the *Dumfries Ms* of

1710. From Lat *aequus* (equal) + *vocare* (to call) to form the verb *equivocare* to OF *equivoque* (F *équivoque*) to ME.

ethereal, of the nature of ether or bright or airy. Stem is Gk *aither* (the upper air, clear sky), hence Gk *aitherios*, Lat *aether* or *ether*. The modern meaning has developed into heavenly.

excrescence, an unnatural or disfiguring growth; figuratively a hump from a flat surface. From Lat *ex* (from) + *cresco* (I grow) forming *excrescentia* through Rom to ME.

fellow, a companion, but can also denote an equal, or even an inferior. *The Regius Ms* 1390, 'Fellow by friendship' and in the *Cooke Ms c* 1450, line 675 *etc* 'Euclid commands that they that were less by wit should not be called servant or subject but Fellow for the nobility of their gentle blood.' Fellow appears frequently after this date *ie* in the *Edinburgh Register House Ms* 1696 and other exps Fellow-

Craft is a Scottish masonic term, possibly
16th century, but only coming into
English Freemasonry in the 1723 *Constitutions*, almost certainly imported by the
author, himself a Scot. The word comes
probably from the AS *folgian* (to follow)
or the Icelandic *felagi, felag*, (companion-
ship), OE *feolage, felow, felan*, or Scottish *fallow*, all meaning approximately
one who shares with another, a partner, to
OE.

fiat, a Lat word meaning 'let it be done',
being the 3rd person singular of the present subjunctive of the verb *fieri* (to hap-
pen). Fiat now means an authoritative
order, as in Genesis 1 v 3; '*Fiat lux*' (Let
there be light).

fire, The discharge of firearms, but the
word also has a special meaning connected with the drinking of toasts. In
medieval times, toasts were sometimes
accompanied by musketry. The origin and
types of fire are given in *AQC* 75.
Masonic drinking procedures first appear

in the F Exp *Reception d'un Frey-Maçon*, 1737 but it is not named as 'fire' until *Le Secret des Francs-Maçons*,, 1742. The first English description of 'fire' as a complement to drinking a toast is in TDK 1760. There is no evidence to decide whether it was started in English or French masonry. The English word comes from the AS *fyr* to the OE *fair* or *fir*.

Garter (Order of), an order of knighthood instituted in 1348 by King Edward III. The sash of the order is the dark blue colour worn by Grand, Provincial, District, Overseas and London rank on their regalia. The light blue colour of other regalia is, perhaps fortuitously, that of the now extinct Order of St Patrick. The first masonic reference to the Order of the Garter is in MD. 1730 as the 'Star and Garter'. The word 'garter' is probably of Celtic or Breton origin as *gar*(leg). In OF there is *garret*, *garet* or *jaret* (bend of the knee or calf of leg) to later French and English *gartier* or *garter*.

gauge (or gage, judge, etc), it now means any instrument for measuring, coming into masonry as an operative tool. A template of an 18 inch 'judge' is in the Aberdeen Lodge Mark book of 1670 and the word appears again in the *Edinburgh Register House Ms* 1696 as 'the common judge'. It later became the 'rule' and the predecessor of the '24 inch gauge'. This, as a Working Tool of the Entered Apprentice, is first found in TDK 1760. No Grand Lodge appears to have adopted decimalization. The etymology is unknown though the word appears in OF as *gauger* (to measure).

gavel, a mason's tool and also a mallet used by a presiding officer to keep order or draw attention. In TDK 1760, the 'common gavel or setting maul' is a Working Tool of the Entered Apprentice. The etymology is unknown but it is *not*, as in the OED, 'of US origin about 1680' as it appears in the YFR 1399 list among masons' tools as '1 big gavel'. This may have been a wedge-shaped axe for trimming stone. Mackey suggests, probably correctly, that there is a connection with the shape of the gable or gavel end of a house, derived from the OHG *gipful* (summit). There are similar early Scandinavian words.

geometry, the link between geometry and architecture causes its association with masonry. This is stressed in the *Old Charges* and early Exps until at one time a 'geometer' became an alternative name for a freemason. The first masonic use of the word 'geometry' is in the *Regius Ms* 1390, which defines the constitutions of masonry as 'the Constitutions of the Art of Geometry according to Euclid'. The word comes from Gk *gé* (earth) + *metrein* (to measure) to form *geometria* and Lat *geometria*, OF *geometrie* to ME.

glimmering, describes a display of a faint or wavering light, thus appropriate to the Third Degree. Probably a word of Scandinavian origin from Swedish *glimai*, Danish *glimre*, *etc*.

gloves, Specimens were found in Tutankhamen's tomb built in the 13th century BC and there have been many allusions in Gk and Lat literature. Pictures show masons wearing gloves of the gauntlet type *c* 1200. As gloves were forbidden, except for nobility, masons presumably had special leave to wear them when working as protection against splinters and lime burning. The Natural History of Staffordshire, 1686, mentions gloves being presented by candidates to brethren and, at Aberdeen in 1670, there was a similar custom. The giving of gloves *to* candidates became common later, particularly on the continent. Masters of lodges may now dispense with gloves in certain circumstances (*Information for the Guidance of Members of the Craft*, 1978, p 21) and gauntlets are optional (p 21). See APRON, also HC 75-7, 180-1 and 319-21. The word comes form the AS *glof*, possibly connected with the OHG word *lof* and other LG words relating to hands.

Golden Fleece, an order of knighthood instituted by Philip the Good, Duke of Burgundy in 1430. The Grandmastership passed by marriage in 1447 to the Habsburgs and the order became the highest honour in Spain and Austria. The badge of the Order was presumably taken from the legend of Jason and the Argonauts. Appears first in masonry in TDK 1760. The English word 'fleece' (the F title is *'Toison d'or'*) is from OE *fleos*, *flys* and similar Germanic words as *fleua*, possibly etymologically connected with Lat *pluma* (a feather).

grip, the OED gives one meaning as 'Masons mystic word'. Grip appears first in the Exp *Sloane Ms* 1700 and constantly afterwards. From AS *gripe* (grasp, clutch) to OHG *grif* and *grippa* (handful).

guard, either a verb or a noun meaning watch over, protection, *etc*. In masonic documents from earliest times. Comes from OF *Garder* (warder) to HG *warten* (watch). See also WARDEN.

hail (-ing), the word came into use about mid 16th century for greetings from a distance, particularly in a nautical context. Used as part of a masonic sign, it is found first in TDK 1760 with no clue to its source. The sign is clearly based either on incidents in Exodus 17 v 8-12 or in Joshua 10 v 6-14. See JOSHUA. The alternative name for the sign as either 'of prayer' or 'of perseverance' is discussed in HC 30-32. The word is derived from Old Norse *heill* (health, prosperity) OE *hailse* (a greeting wishing health).

hele (or heal, heill, heil), this is an old dialect word in SW England, now obsolescent, except in a few rural areas. Its first appearance in masonry seems to be the *Harleian Ms c* 1650, now in the British Library. It also is later in the *Edinburgh Register House Ms* 1696, as '*heill*'. Dictionaries say that it should be pronounced 'heel' but in Emulation working, 'hail' is correct. The OE word was *helian* or *helan* (to cover).

hecatomb, means the sacrifice of a large number of animals. The word appears in the additional address to the Immediate Past Master, describing his jewel, the 47th Problem of Euclid. This was the most important discovery of Pythagoras, who is reported to have exclaimed 'Eureka' and to have sacrificed a hecatomb. Another myth connected with *Eureka* refers to Archimedes but the word, roughly meaning 'Got it' could be ascribed to any discovery. The word is Gk and formed from *ekaton* (100) + *bous* (ox).

The 47th Proposition of Euclid is demonstrated by the Past Master's jewel.

Hiram, this is the Hebrew form of the Phoenician name 'Huram' (nobly born) and is possibly also an abbreviation or the equivalent of Ahiram (Numbers 26 v 38) meaning 'my brother'. Early writers state that a daughter of Hiram, King of Tyre, was married to Solomon, hence the close alliance. Extensive literature exists on the craftsman who appears under various spellings in the *Old Charges* and who also had this name. Preston uses the word for the master's gavel and, in the USA the word appears to be a normal one for a gavel.

hoodwink, blindfolding candidates was normal procedure in the ancient mysteries and medieval initiations into secret societies. The early masonic mentions of blindfolding candidates are in several English Exps of *c* 1723 *et seq.* The Scottish mention of the word is later. The actual word 'hoodwink' is first used in TDK 1760 and again in Preston. It comes from two OE words *hod* (hood) + *wincian* (to wink) indicating that the hood, a usual part of medieval dress, was pulled over the eyes to blind or deceive the wearer.

immemorial, reaching back beyond memory. Used masonically to designate lodges etc existing before their parent bodies were formed. From Lat *im* (the euphonic version of the prefix *in*) + *memoria* (mindful) to OF *memor*.

indite, to put into words or writing. As used in the ritual, it is an example of the tautology of the period; repetition being for emphasis even though the meaning is amply covered by other words in the same sentence. From Lat *in* (a suffix meaning in) + *dicere* (to say) to ME through OF.

initiate, the word used by the Romans to describe admission to their secret or sacred societies. Similar words appear in most Rom and came into use in ME about the end of the 16th century. Later in the same century, the word was adopted by masonry, replacing the earlier 'making' or 'to make'. The Lat past participle of the verb *initiare* (to begin) produced *initiatus*.

insidious, the normal use is as an adjective meaning treacherous or by a secret procedure etc. The word's use as a noun seems to be purely masonic. From Lat *insidiae* (an ambush) with the verb *insidiere* to *insidosus*.

install (-ation), to invest with an office or dignity by placing the recipient into an official seat or stall. First masonic use seems to have been in the ceremony of consecration described in the 1723 *Constitutions*. In this, the new master and wardens are installed. From L Lat *in* (in) + *stallum* (seat) to *installare* and OF *installer* to ME.

Jerusalem, derived from the Gk *Hierosolyma*, in its turn from the Hebrew *Yeroushalum*, often translated as 'city of peace'. In fact, this is the name of a town on Mount Ophel, a short distance from the actual city which King David captured from the Jebusites. This was called *Urusalimu* meaning 'a city dedicated to Shalem' (a Jebusite God).

jewel, building tools, first appearing in the *Edinburgh Register House Ms* 1696, are listed as 'fixed or moveable' jewels. Later Exp and catechisms vary considerably as to what were the jewels of a lodge. Personal jewels worn by officers date from 1727 when Grand Lodge ordered all masters and wardens to wear them. The wearing of jewels by other officers is mentioned in TDK 1760. Further jewels have been authorized from time to time, the latest being the TROWEL worn by the lodge Charity Steward. The word jewel is based on the Lat *jocus* (jest, game or sport), OF *joil, iuel, iouel*, diminutives of *joie* (joy).

Joppa, one of the oldest cities in the world, dating from about 5,000 BC. It is some 35 miles west of Jerusalem and had the only natural harbour in the area. For this reason, it was used for landing the

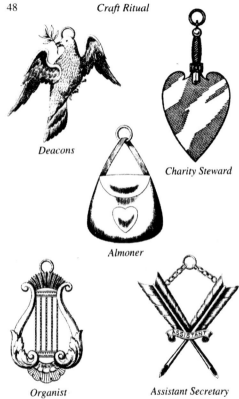

Deacons

Charity Steward

Almoner

Organist

Assistant Secretary

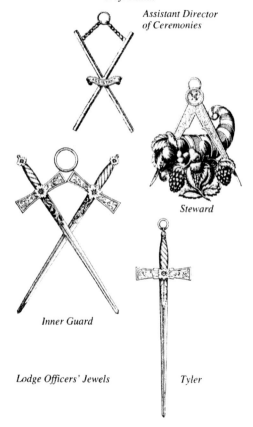

Assistant Director of Ceremonies

Steward

Inner Guard

Lodge Officers' Jewels

Tyler

cedars, floated down from Tyre, which were used in the building of the Temple (2 Chronicles 2 v 16). Now part of Tel Aviv. The Hebrew name was Yaffa, meaning 'beautiful'. In Gk *ioppé*.

Joshua, one of Moses's generals, and succeeded him as the leader of the Israelites. A part of the Second Degree sign is attributed to him; his prayer to God to continue the daylight is recorded in Joshua 10 v 6-14 but the sign is not mentioned. Some form of sign was given by Moses (Exodus 17 v 8-12) while Joshua defeated the Amalekites. See also HAIL. Joshua's name in the Bible is a Hebrew version of *Yehoshua* meaning 'redemption' or 'God is my saviour'.

labour, except when it is temporarily 'called off', a lodge is 'at labour' from its opening to its closing. 'Labour' as opposed to 'REFRESHMENT' appears in TDK 1760. Lat *labor* (toil, exertion, effort, trouble) to OF *labour* but in F is only used to describe ploughing. It is, however, the basis for the ME word describing hard work of any kind.

landmark, the importance of landmarks dates from time immemorial but masonically no earlier than the 1723 *Constitutions* which lay down that masonic landmarks are immutable. Some Grand Lodges lay down lists of their landmarks; the British do not. The subject has been much discussed. See Mackey, FGC 332-7 and HC 362-5. The word comes from the OE *land* (land) + *mearc* (mark).

level, an operative building tool. It is shown first as a Freemason's tool in the Aberdeen Lodge mark book of 1670. From about 1725 the word appears in various Exps as a lodge 'light' or 'jewel' (Moveable in MD 1730). Was worn as a personal jewel by the Senior Warden in TDK 1760 but is not classed as a Working Tool until the Union, 1813. Lat *libra* (balance) has a diminutive *libella*. OF *livel* (now *niveau*) to ME *level*, *livel*.

Lewis, the masonic term for the uniniti-
ated son of a Freemason. The word
appears in the *Wilkinson Ms* 1727 and is
in the Deputy Grand Master's Song in
the 1738 *Constitutions*. Lewises have
varying privileges depending on the con-
stitution. The non-masonic meaning is
that of a lifting device for stone. The etymology is confused, possibly from the
name Louis or Lewis. See FGC 414-19
and *Early Masonic Catechisms* 1963 Ed
144-9.

lily, lily-work enriched the pillars of the
Temple according to the Explanation of
the Second Degree Tracing Board. Lily-
work appears in the Bible (1 Kings 7 v 22)
for the pillars and is mentioned in Josephus's *Antiquities of the Jews*, Book VIII,
Chap III. In 2 Chronicles 4 v 5, the molten
sea is decorated with 'flowers of lilies' but
not the pillars. Plants of the lily family
appear to be translations of the Hebrew
susan, sosan or *soannah*. The references
in the Song of Solomon (Chap 2 v 1-2 and
16) may allude to the Madonna lily but, in

Chapter 5 v 13, describing lips, the red anemone seems more likely. Lily, as a word, comes from the Gk *leiron* and Lat *lilium* but both may have an earlier Mediterranean origin. See LOTUS and *AQC* 94.

lodge, the word has three meanings — a room or building where Freemasons meet; the society of men who meet there; and the meeting of that body. The first mention of 'lodge' seems to be in the *Vale Abbey Records*, 1278, but the word is certainly earlier. The Germanic *laube* (leaf or arbour) is the probable source of the OE *loggia* (to inhabit) and *loge* or *logga* (temporary dwellings). The Italian word *loggia* (a gallery) produced the Rom *loge* (room or box). When Freemasonry reached the Continent about 1725, French masons adopted their existing word *loge*, which was, and still is, a box in a theatre or dressing room as the equivalent of the English word 'lodge'. See FGC 35 and Mackey, though the latter is faulty etymologically.

lotus, it is suggested that the water-lily or lotus of Egypt and Asia (*nymphaea lotus*) was the lily described as decorating the Temple (See LILY). There was much Egyptian influence in architecture and the lotus appears on hieroglyphics. The lotus used by the *Lotophagi* (lotus-eaters of Homer's *Odyssey*) to produce a loss of all desire to return home may in fact have been a tree. The word comes from the Gk *lotus* and Lat *lotus,* both words being of Semitic origin. See *AQC* 94.

lyre, an ancient harp-like instrument. It is named in the optional address to the lodge organist. A Rom word from the Gk *lura,* Lat *lyra.*

mason, there have been many fanciful theories about this word, but the etymology is straightforward. A mason is a man who cuts stone. The Rom root is the Lat *macio* or *mattio.* The word can be found in Old Norman F as *machun* and Old Central F as *macon.* There were varieties of the word in England as early as the 11th century. By

1400, it was appearing in the *Romance of the Rose* as *massoun* and Caxton was printing it in its present form in 1489. It is possible that there is a connection with the OHG *mezzo* (to hew). See FGC 145. The extension to 'freemason' is much more complicated and has been studied on paper many times but there seems to be no firm answer. See *AQC* 2, 10, 11, 48, 65 and numerous other sources. The writer favours a Templar origin of as early a date as the 11th century. Artisans working for the Templars called themselves 'free' and had an international status of freedom from local taxes wherever they worked. Templar 'freemasons' built the Temple in Fleet Street in London and other buildings in the 12th century. English masons, at the same time, did not belong to local guilds but travelled to construction sites as they were needed. Having no 'domicile' they, like the Templar artisans, would not pay taxes.

master, the title describes the head of an organization. This would include the heads of lodges, operative or speculative.

Some lodges used other terms but, certainly in England master was usual. The basis is Lat *magnus* (great) to *magister*; to ME through OF *meistrier*. Modern F is *maître*. Rom languages had a similar word which may have come into England before ME began to develop.

maul, (or Beetle) appears in the YFR 1399 as a heavy hammer of any kind. Later, in the *Whole Institute of Masonry* 1724, the maul is a 'lodge light'. It was also used by the three ruffians as a 'setting maul' in MD 1730, and again in TDK 1760 both as a 'gavel or setting maul' and a 'lodge light'. Preston calls it a 'mallet' about 1800. In English masonry, unlike in many other Grand Lodges, the gavel and the maul have different uses. In some Grand Lodges, the master's tool is a maul. The word comes from Lat *malleus* (hammer), through OF *mail* possibly into OE as *maul*, *mell* or *mail*. The word 'beetle' from Old Saxon *bietel*, OE *betel*, from *beatan* (to beat) was a word for any tool with a heavy head and was used alternately with maul, as in MD 1730, where it is called a 'setting beadle'. An early Exp of 1726 advertised '*The Whole History of a Widow's Son killed by a Blow of a Beetle.*

mercenary, it means working for money or other reward or actuated by self-interest. The Lat *mercenarius*, the adjective from *merces* (thanks, reward) came through OF into ME early in the 16th century. The English word 'mercy' and the F word *merçi* (thanks) are from the same root.

menatchin, the word does not appear in the Bible where the Hebrew word, which means leader, head or conductor is translated as 'Solomon's officers'. In 1 Kings 5 v 16, there are 3,300; in 2 Chronicles 2 v 18, they are called 'overseers' and number 3,600.

meridian, this is the point in the sky at which a star or planet reaches its highest altitude — in the case of the sun, at noon.

In the northern hemisphere, this is in the south and represents the Junior Warden in a lodge. The word is first mentioned masonically in the Exp *Institution of Freemasonry* 1725. It is derived from Lat *medius* (middle) + *dies* (day) becoming *meridianus* to OF *meridien* to late ME.

morality, the modern meaning is 'possessing a moral lesson or having the ability to distinguish between right and wrong' (OED). 'A Mason is obliged by his tenure to obey the moral law' (*1723 Constitutions*). From Lat *mos*, plural *mores* (manner or custom) producing *moralia* and *moralitas*. To OF *morel*, *morale*, *moralité*, all meaning morality, to ME.

mosaic, in the *Edinburgh Register House Ms* 1696, and some other early Exps there is a 'square pavement' as a 'jewel of the lodge'. The words Mosaik pavement appear in the *Wilkinson Ms* 1727 and MD 1730, as moveable jewels 'for the Master to draw his design upon', thus suggesting some form of tracing board. This seems reasonable and would fit in with the practice of the candidate obliterating the floor drawings after his initiation, something that continued certainly until 1779. A special squared carpet for a lodge seems unlikely while lodges used taverns as their meeting places. Thus the question how the early 'Mosaick pavement' turned into the present lodge squared carpet is unsolved. Several theories exist but the present use of the latter seems to have started with Preston. However, see FGC 132 and Mackey. The word probably comes from the Gk *mouseton* (the place consecrated to the Nine Muses). C Lat *mousa* (muse) to *mosaicus* (a pavement of small stones in a pattern), Italian *musaico,* OF *mosaique* to ME. No connection with Moses.

mote, there are three words 'mote', all from AS, with different meanings. The masonic word 'mote' is the third person singular of the present subjunctive of the v *motan* (to be allowed, to permit) thus 'so mote it be' is an old form of 'amen' which means 'so let it be'. Masons have retained the first form which has died out elsewhere. The two other meanings of 'mote' are an 'assembly', now archaic, and a minute object. (Matthew 7 v 3, and Luke 6 v 41). The etymology of all three words is different.

mystery,   the meaning depends on the sources of this word. Gk *misterion* (to close the eyes or lips, hence to preserve a secret), became Lat *misterium* and, through OF *mystere* (now *mystère*) to ME *misterie* and modern English *mystery* for something unknown or unexplained. OF *metier* and AS *mister*, *misterie* (all meaning trade) became ME *mystery* or *mistery*. Confusion of the two derivations has produced the masonic phrase 'secrets or mysteries' which is an unnecessary repetition unless 'mysteries' is accepted in its archaic meaning of 'trade or skill.'

network,   normally means any material used to form a net, and is derived from OE *net(t)* and similar old Saxon or Germanic words. In 1 Kings v 18 etc 'network' is a translation of the Hebrew *sebaka* interpreted in several ways but usually by seven strands of interlocking links of chain enveloping the round pommels at the top of the CHAPITERS of the Temple PILLARS. From these hung the golden POMEGRANATES which covered the upper parts of the LILYWORK (or LOTUS flowers). The word is to be found in a masonic context in MD 1730. See also *AQC* 94 and HC 111-2.

obligation, an obligation is the binding of a person by an oath. In the masonic sense, it binds the Freemason to the Order. The word came late into masonry (*Wilkinson Ms* 1727 and MD 1730). Previously it was oaths that were sworn. From Lat *ob* (about) + *ligo* (bind) give the verb *obligare* (to render indebted). Developed through OF into ME and in use before *c* 1500.

olive, symbolically an emblem of peace. The present jewel of the DEACON, with the DOVE holding the olive branch, dates

from the Union of 1813. Earlier it had been
the compass (*Jachin and Boaz* 1762) or the
figures of Mercury holding a *caduceus* (herald's staff). English lodges of pre-Union
date may continue to use the Mercury but
may not replace it. From Gk *olaiva*, botani-
cally *olea europaea*. The words 'oil' and F
huile are derived from the word.

operative, a person employed as a worker.
In Freemasonry, an operative is the opposite to a SPECULATIVE. MD refers to an
operative mason but later TDK 1760
reverts to 'working masons'. The basic
stem is Lat *opus* (work) through *operatio*
and various derivatives.

opulence, possessing riches or affluent.
Lat *opes* (wealth, resources) giving *opu-
lens* and *opulentia* (possessing wealth).
The word came from OF into ME at the
end of the 16th century.

ostensible, offered as real, or having the
character represented; seeming; professed
or pretended. Often implied as opposed to

actual. In some rituals, it is the duty of the Junior Warden 'as ostensible steward of the lodge' to guide the actual stewards in their duties. From Lat *ob* (about) + *tendere* (to stretch), giving *ostentus*. Through OF *ostensible* to ME about the mid-18th century.

paradox, a sentence seemingly self-contradictory or absurd, through possibly well-founded or true. From the Gk *para* (alongside) + *doxa* (opinion) gives *paradoxon* (incredible) to OF *paradoxe* to ME.

parallelopipedon, in the lecture on the First Degree Tracing Board. A parallelogram is a four-sided rectangle and a parallelopipedon is a solid figure contained by a number of parallelograms, usually six. The word is formed from the Gk *para* (alongside) + *allelos* (one another) + *epi* (upon) + *pedon* (ground). A more correct spelling is parallel*e*pipedon.

pass, the word was first used as a masonic degree step in the *Graham Ms* 1726.

Mackey aptly suggests that it alludes to the Fellowcraft 'passing through the middle chamber of the Temple, the place where the FCs received their wages'. In early masonic Mss, the Past Masters were known as 'pass masters', the same etymology applying to one who has passed the degree. Lat *passus* (step or grade). Through Rom languages to *passer* (to pass) to ME.

pencil, it is not known when the pencil, now a Third Degree Working Tool, first came into masonry but it is possible that it was in the late 18th century. The pencil is not used masonically in the USA. The Lat *penicillus* (painter's brush) is a diminutive of *penis* (tail). The word came into late ME as *pensel* through OF *pince* (paint brush, now *pinceau*).

perpendicular, upright or, more technically, at right angles to the plane of the horizon. The word is used for the depth of a grave in the Third Degree but it first appears in MD 1730 as a recognition sign for masons, *ie* 'All Squares, Angles and Perpendiculars'. It comes from the Lat *per* (through) + *pendere* (to hang or weigh) to *perpendiculum* (a PLUM-LINE). The archaic word 'perpend-ashlar' appearing in early Exps as a double ashlar, through others and so binding them, is an equally correct derivation from Lat.

pillar, (column), a firm, upright separate support. Free standing pillars or columns were normal architectural features in the Near East in Biblical times. Two sets are named in the ritual:

a. The pillars of the Temple were probably called by the first words or oracles giving power to the Davidian dynasty as 'Yahweh will establish (Yakin) thy kingdom for ever' and 'in the strength (Boaz) of Yahweh will thy kingdom reign'. Reference to these pillars has been found in a letter dated 1691, written by a Scottish Minister (*Genesis of Freemasonry* 1978 by Knoop and Jones) but their first appearance in ritual is in the *Edinburgh Register House*

Ms 1696. It is not until TDK 1760 that they are referred to as columns for the wardens. (The Bible references are 1 Kings 7 v 21 and 2 Chron 3 v 17). Jachin, the Assistant High Priest, assisting at the Temple dedication is a masonic myth.

b. The three pillars, Strength, Beauty and Wisdom which 'support the Lodge' date from the *Wilkinson Ms* 1727 but die out to reappear in the Lecture on the First Degree Tracing Board.

The word is derived from Lat *pila* (pointed stick or post), OF *pilier* to ME *piler*, *pile* developing into *pilar* and eventually *pillar*.

plumb, the plumb is named among the masons' tools in the YFR 1399 but naturally had been in use much earlier (See Amos 7 v 7). It was a lodge 'light' or 'jewel' in Exps from 1724 but, though worn as a personal jewel by the Junior Warden in TDK 1760, and presumably in subsequent lodge meetings, it is not otherwise mentioned until it became a Working

Tool of the Second Degree at the Union, 1813. The Junior Warden's jewel was known as the 'plumb' as late as the 1861 *Book of Constitutions*. The word plumb (or plum-rule, plumb-line, plummet, etc) is derived from Lat *plumbum* (lead) to ME through OF *plumb*.

pomegranate, the 'pomegranates' on the Temple PILLARS are translations of Hebrew meaning 'circular crowns'. The *Septuagint* has the Gk *epithemata choneuta* (cast additions) while the *Vulgate* has Lat *furniculus capitellorum* or *capitai* (round pommels or tops). The Hebrew for pomegranate is *rimmonim* and is found in several Biblical place names as in Judges 20 v 47 and Joshua 19 v 13. The English word 'pomegranate' of the *Authorised Version* is of Lat derivation, *pomus granata* (seedy apple). The word appears in masonic ms in MD 1730.

porch (-way), in MD 1730, the porch is a 'master jewel'. Preston uses the word as an ornament of a Master Mason's lodge as in the present ritual. The word 'porchway' used in the First Degree seems to be a masonic invention. From *porta* (door), then *porticus* (colonnade, gallery, porch) to OF *porche*, to ME.

prefect, the rank must have been used during the Roman occupation of Britain but presumably fell out of use when that ended. It seems to have returned with a Rom or OF derivation as *prefect* (now prefet) to ME From the Lat *prae* (over) + *facere* (to make) to *praefectus* (an overseer, etc).

principle, a principle is stronger than a TENET as it is a primary element, force or law which produces or determines results. It is thus the ultimate basis on which the existence of something depends. The word is in the *Sloan Ms* 1700, as 'from whom do you derive your principalls?'. Preston refers to the 'Grand Principles of the Order'. From Lat *primus* (first) + *cipe* (from *capare* to hold) gives *principia* foundations, principles etc. OF *principe* to ME.

raise, used in its present sense in the *Graham MS* 1726, and after 1760 is common. However, as late as 1825, Preston uses 'exaltation'. From Old Norse *raisa*, OE *raevah* (to set upright or lift) HC 230-1.

ravening, it is sometimes given as 'ravenous' but the distinction is immaterial as both words are based on the Lat *rapere* (to seize, tear, take by force) giving *rapina* (robbery, prey etc). OF *raviner* to OE as rape, ravish etc. There are various meanings such as 'to devour voraciously' or 'be excessively hungry'. *Jachin & Boaz* 1762, gives 'vultures of the air' in the ritual while Preston uses 'ravenous vultures). The word 'raven' is based on OE and has no connection. HC 372-3.

rectitude, uprightness in PRINCIPLES and conduct. From Lat *rectus* go straight, upright) to L Lat *rectitudo* (rightness) to ME through Rom.

refreshment, in the 17th century, the word only applied to food and drink but later, in TDK 1760, it became associated with a temporary stopping of LABOUR. In this sense, it is becoming archaic, except in masonry. From Lat *re* (again) + Lat *friscus* (fresh or new). The Lat root produced other OF words which came into ME. It may also be derived from OHG *frisc* (fresh).

regulation, a rule prescribed for conduct or action. Regulations for masonry are noted in the Exp *Shibboleth* 1765, as having been written in 1663. From *regere* (to rule) to *regula* (a rule, example etc) with past participle, probably only in L Lat *regulatus*, thence through Rom to ME.

relief, the word has many meanings. In the masonic sense, it implies 'an easing or taking care of the cause of distress'. With brotherly love and truth, relief is one of the three basic masonic PRINCIPLES. It is discussed at length in a CHARGE given by Thomas Dunckerley (7.9.1769) which appears in *Candid Disquisitions* 1769 by Wellins Calcott. From Lat *re* (again) + *levare* (to raise) or *levis* (light) to OF *relever* to ME *releve*, *relief*.

repository, refers to any vessel, receptacle, chamber, store, etc used for storage. From the past participle of Lat verb *reponere* (to put something back in its place) producing *repositorium*. OF *repositoire* (modern *réposoir*) to ME about 1600.

rite, in modern use, a rite is normally of a religious or mystical nature while a ceremony may be entirely secular. Some thirty masonic rites are known of which less than half are now worked. From Lat *ritus* (usage) to OF *rit*, *rite* to ME as a formal procedure, custom or practice of a solemn or formal kind.

Roman Eagle, the figure of an eagle on a staff was, from about 200 BC, the sign of a Roman legion, corresponding to the colours of a modern military unit. As such, it was highly honoured. The word 'eagle' is from the Lat *aquila* through OF *aigle* to ME. The phrase appears first in masonry in TDK 1760.

saltire, adopted as a heraldic term for something in the shape of a St Andrew's Cross. The word appears first to describe jewels of the officers of a lodge in the 1883 *Book of Constitutions*. Previously the word 'crossed' was used. From Lat v *saltire* (to leap suggesting an abrupt change). Through OF *sautoir*, *sauteur* (a jumper or change of direction) into ME originally as *sawtire*.

scene, the usual word for a Gk or Lat theatre stage. From Gk *skene* (a tent, booth or stage). Lat *scena*, *scaena* to OF *scene* into ME where it developed into the word for any place where action might take place.

scruple, the smallest division of the Roman coinage. Through the Rom the word has developed in ME to a 'small thought or worry that troubles the mind', a doubt or hesitation. From Lat *scruplus*, the diminutive of *scrupus* (a small, sharp or pointed stone).

sepulchre (or sepulture), OED gives both words as having the meaning of 'an interment or burial' but considers the latter to be archaic. Sepulchre, as a 'tomb or burial place' is also becoming somewhat old-fashioned, except for certain idiomatic phrases such as 'a whited sepulchre' or the name of Christ's burial place, and may also soon become obsolete. Sepulchre comes from the past participle of the Lat v *sepelire* (to bury) which gives *sepulchrum* to OF *sepulchre* and a similar word in ME Sepulture is from the same Lat stem to *sepulture* to OF *sepulture* and so to ME. HC 184-6 gives a somewhat artificial differentiation between the two words.

shibboleth, the Hebrew word *sibbolet* (pronounced *shibboleth*) means an ear of corn. In the Semitic dialect used by the Ephraimites this was pronounced *sibboleth ie* without the 'sh'. The result is the story in Judges 12 v 6 and the word becoming a synonym for a password. A similar word appears in Psalm 69 v 2 and Isaiah 44 v 3 meaning a stream in flood. The word Shibboleth appears first masonically in a F Exp dated 1745 with the story of the Book of Judges in a later Exp in 1747. There is no evidence that the masonic association began with French masons and the word appears in TDK 1760. The combination of the meanings of the two similar words, given in the explanation of the Second Degree Tracing Board, is etymologically incorrect. The mistake seems to have started in the Exp *Jachin & Boaz* 1762 which, in a footnote, gives the meaning of Shibboleth as 'plenty'. 'An ear of corn near to a fall of water' — a duplication of two similar words — was the result.

skirret, the word first appears in a masonic context in a letter of 24 Sep 1816 as the 'schivit line'. It is only used in English masonry and may be an old dialect gardening or building word for the swivel on which a line is wound — the line being the important symbolic element. This appears in the Exp the *Whole Institution of Masonry* 1724. The etymology is unknown and seems to have no possible connection with the vegetable called 'skirret'. Many derivations have been suggested, none particularly satisfactory. HC 148, FGC 45-6 and a *Commentary on the Masonic Ritual* by Dr E. H. Cartright 196. The word does not appear in Preston so presumably was introduced at the Union 1813.

slip, is first used masonically in MD 1730. In the 1760s, the word is 'slipped'. The decay theme, which already had occurred in the *Graham Ms* 1726 and which persisted in Continental masonry, is missing from Preston but reappears at the Union. It is used in Scotland but only in some US Grand Lodges. Mackey suggests incorrectly that the idea was of recent origin, dating from about 1840. The word comes from OE *slupan* and ME *slippen* (to slip).

slipshod, wearing shoes down at the heels. The first masonic mention of uncovered feet is in the *Graham Ms* 1726, 'nor cloathed shod nor bairfoot' but not found again until the *Essex Ms* 1750 as 'nor naked shod nor barefoot'. As 'barefoot nor shod', it is in TDK 1760 and usually in manuscripts after that date. The word 'slipshod' seems to have been first used by Preston. Many non-masonic ceremonies have included the baring of the feet. From SLIP (*qv*) + OE *shod*, past participle of OE *shoe* (to put on a shoe).

solicitation, to ask for earnestly, to entreat. From Lat *solum* (whole, entire) + *citum* (past participle of the verb *ciere* [to put in motion]). This gives *solicitare* (to stir up or agitate), OF *sollicitation* to OE developing into its present meaning. For a note on 'improper solicitation' see HC 129-34 but a speech by the Grand Master recently suggests the masonic view is unnecessarily rigid.

Solomon, the 10th son of David, the second by Bathsheba, 3rd King of Israel (BC 978-938). His traditional and biblical story is too well known to need repeating. Hebrew, *Shelomo*; Gk and F *Salomon*; Arabic, *Suliman*. All mean 'peaceful'.

speculative, the OED defines to 'speculate' as 'to indulge in thought of a conjectural theoretical nature'. The word was used by the writers Addison and Steele in their paper, *The Spectator*, as an adjective, possibly causing it to become common usage. The earliest example of the word may be in Preston's Second Degree Lecture but the word was certainly used much earlier by masons to describe themselves. Only in Freemasonry is the word now used as a noun; the modern form being speculator which usually has a financial implication. From Lat *spectare* (to look), through *specula* (a watchtower) gives *speculator* (one who looks) to ME.

sport, amuse oneself with or by. In the First Degree Charity Charge. Is an abbreviation of disport. Lat *de* (away) + *porto* (carry). To ME through OF.

square, a common tool with a symbolic meaning from the earliest times — not restricted to masonry — for being honest or upright. The square takes its present place in masonry as a Working Tool in TDK 1760 but appears often in earlier mss as a lodge 'light' or 'decoration'. From Lat *ex* (out) + *quattuor* (four) to *quadra* (four-cornered) to *exquadra* gave OF *esquare*, *esquarre* (F *équerre*) to ME *squire*, *square*.

steward, in Freemasonry, stewards originated from brethren who helped to organize the annual grand feast, probably first in 1721. Shortly after, there were stewards in private lodges. As many lodges had no deacons, the steward's duties, until the Union 1813, included ceremonial work in lodge. From AS *stig* (house or dwelling place — sty is of the same origin) + *weard* (ward or guardian) gave *stigweard*, *stiweard* or *steward* as the manager, usually of a property.

sublime, the word appeared first in Irish masonry about 1754 and, in English masonry, to describe the Third Degree, about 1763. It was adopted into the ritual at the Union 1813, almost certainly through the influence of the Grand Lodge of the Ancients. The word is much used in Continental masonry, especially in the Ancient and Accepted Rite. Lat *sublimis* (lofty), possibly based upon *sub* (up to) + *limes* (boundary) or *limen* (lintel). OF *sublime* to ME.

superstructure, any part of a building considered in relation to the part on which it rests. The word is in the Charity Charge to the Entered Apprentice in the ritual after the Union, 1813. It also comes in Preston's First Degree but in a different context. From Lat *super* (Over) + *struere* (to build) thence through Rom languages to ME.

symbol (-ic), the word means something that stands for or represents something else. It appears frequently in masonry, but early masonic writers seem to have considered a symbol as more theoretical than the possibly tangible EMBLEM. Such differentiation is dying out and the words are more or less synonymous. From the Gk *syn* (together, alike etc) + *ballo* (to throw) give *symbolon* or *sumbolos*. The word came into ME through Rom words, such as the F *symbolique*.

temperance, while the word temper has retained its meaning of treating metals and calming the mind, 'temperance' has developed into the practice of restraint, usually in connection with eating or drinking. In its wider sense, as in masonry, it retains its meaning as one of the cardinal virtues, with Prudence, Fortitude and Justice. See *The Spirit of Masonry*, 1775, by William Hutchinson, 115. The past participle of the Lat v *temperare* (to mix, mingle, restrain) gives *temperatus*, the root being *tempus* (time). The word appears in early Saxon but, during the development of English from ME it was probably influenced by the OF *temprer* or *tremper* (F *tempérer* to moderate).

tenet, from about 1600, the word applied to any opinion but it is now defined in the OED as a 'doctrine, dogma, principle or opinion in religion, politics, philosophy or the like, held by a school, sect, party or person'. Preston refers to the 'grand tenets of the institution', *c* 1807. The third person singular of the Lat v *tenere* (to hold) gives *tenet* (he holds). Through OF to ME.

tessellated, the word means in the style of checkered MOSAIC work. In Freemasonry, the word is suggested in some early Exps but only appears in the ritual in the lecture on the First Degree Tracing Board as the edging to the lodge carpet. Many lodges have tessellated edges to their carpets but the reasons are obscure. The subject is fully, but inconclusively discussed in Mackey, FGG 398-9 and HC 321-4. The Lat word *tesselatus* (chequered) is the diminutive of the noun *tessera* (a small cube of stone). The Gk root is *tessares* (four-sided or four).

token, appears in the *Sloan Ms* 1700, used alternatively with GRIP. The word appears in a *Mason's Examination* 1723, with a Hebrew scrip denoting *Roshem* (a symbol or token). The Hebrew word *otn* is used Biblically for token as 'the rainbow shall be a token of a covenant between me and the earth.' (Genesis 9 v 13.) Token, used with Grip, seems to date from the Union, 1813. AS *tacn* or *tacon* (sign, type or representation) from *taecen*, the verb from which teach is derived). Neither the French or German masons use a similar word but have *attouchement* or *griff* to cover both words.

tow, (cable-), a 'cable-rope' is first noted in the *Sloan* Ms 1700. Later Exps called it a 'tow-line' or other similar phrases. It is 'cable-tow' in TDK and subsequently.

Developed from the Old Saxon or Norse *tou* (spin) or *towlic* (fit for spinning) + *cable,* OF derived from the Lat verb *capere* (to take hold of). In ME 1600, there was a cable of spun fibre. The expression 'cable-tow' does not appear in dictionaries as it is purely masonic. The word has no connection with 'tow' (to drag or pull) from which the modern word 'tug' is derived. This comes from the OE *togian.* Thus any idea of a rope used for pulling, rather than restraining, is incorrect.

tracing (-board), the first mention is in YFR 1399 as 'tracy bordes'. Early boards were used for drawing plans; sometimes a squared pavement was used as in *A Mason's Confession* 1727, 'for the master-mason to draw his ground-draughts upon', the *Wilkinson MS* 1727, 'the Mosaik Pavement for the Master to draw his design upon' or MD 1730, using the word 'Trasel-Board'. However, modern lodge boards are not a development of these. They are descended from the diagrams drawn upon the floor of the lodge by the tyler when degrees were conferred. The diagrams were the emblem of the degrees, including the 'tracing-board' for the First and Second Degrees. These chalk or charcoal drawings were first replaced by templets, then by painted cloths and, during the late 18th century, by 'tracing boards'. See *AQC* 6, 29 and 76. The word is derived from the Lat *tractus* (from the v *trahere* to draw). OF *tracier* to ME.

trowel, the word appears first in the rather questionable Exp *The Grand Mystery Laid Open* 1726 and, though it does not appear in the Union ritual, it was an instrument of importance in many of the old lodges and it still figures in some rituals. A F Exp of 1742 gives the trowel importance and connects it with the Master Mason's degree. It is now an essential element in some Continental and some US Grand Lodges. It has lately been reinstated in English masonry as the jewel of the lodge charity steward. Lat *truella* (ladle, scoop) a diminutive of *trua*, (a spoon or ladle), OF (and modern) *truelle* to ME *truel*.

Tubal-Cain, a patriarch named in Genesis 4 v 22 as 'an instructor of every artificer in brass and iron'. Josephus, the Jewish historian says that he invented brass (probably meaning bronze). He is named in the *Cooke Ms* of the 15th century and in most subsequent *Old Charges*. The name was taken as a pass-word in the F Exp *L'Ordre des Francs-Maçons Trahi* 1745 but it was possibly already a significant word as early as 1738 (AQC 84, p 83). It is a pass-word in TDK 1760, and in subsequent Exps Preston mentions a pass-word but does not name it. The meaning 'worldly possessions' given at the Union may be based on a grammatically incorrect combination of the Hebrew *tebel* (earth) and *kanah* (to acquire possessions). The French substituted Peleg (Genesis 10 v 24) towards the end of the 18th century because of a rather fanciful connection between Tubal-Cain and the heathen god of war Vulcan.

tyler (tiler), the title first appears in Freemasonry about 1731; previously the officer in Grand Lodge was called 'porter', 'doorkeeper' or 'garder'. 'Tyler' was probably adopted in masonry as a tiler, by his trade, covered a building and made it secure. The word 'tiler' is in the Exp *The Dialogue between Simon and Peter* 1740, and in Preston. The word with a 'y' is now only used in British masonry; the US masons using 'tiler', as do British tradesmen. A famous tyler in history was Wat Tyler who led a rebellion in 1391. From Lat *tegere* (to cover) and *tego* (a cover), AS *tigele* (a tile). The ME 'tyler' may have been influenced by the 13th century OF *tuile* in reaching its present form.

variance, a state or fact of disagreeing, hence dissension, discord. The suggestion of variance between members having to be settled before entry to a lodge appears first in the later editions of Preston, so may have been in the ritual at the time of the Union, 1813. From Lat *variare* (to differ) to OF *varier, variare* to ME.

wand, a thin stick used for ceremonial purposes as a mark of authority. Early wands may have been associated with the *caduceus* of the god Hermes (Mercury) in his herald or messenger role. Wands were carried in masonry early in the 18th century and are shown in illustrations of F Exps dated about 1745. There are complete references to wands in TDK 1760 and in *Jachin and Boaz* 1762. The word comes from the Old Norse *wandur*, Gothic *wandus* to ME *wand* or *wend*.

warden, the word came into masonry through early trade associations which had wardens by royal charter. The Scottish *Schaw Statutes* 1598, refer to presiding officers as wardens. English lodges had wardens before 1646. The word is an extension of OE *ward* (guard, in charge of, etc). OF varieties as *warain*, *gardein*, developed into OE *weard*, *weardian* to produce ME *wardein* and later warden. Continental masonry uses a different word based on Lat *super* (over) + *videve* (to look) as, in France *surveillant* or, in Italy, *sorveglianti*.

warrant, the word, in English, dates from at least 1450 but was only used in masonry after 1717. A warrant gives authority to perform a specific act *ie* in masonry to hold a lodge. See CHARTER. Very early lodges worked under time immemorial powers or by dispensations, though warrants of confirmation were sometimes issued by Grand Lodge to regularize such lodges. From OF *warantir* (to guard), a variety of the Rom *garant*, the same root as WARDEN and the HG *gewahran* (to certify).

worshipful, the titles 'Worshipful'. 'Right Worshipful' etc are very early civil titles which probably came into masonry about the Grand Lodge era 1717 but which have been used as a mark of respect in the civilian world much earlier. The fact that the word 'worship' is now used in a religious sense has no significance as far as the civil or masonic titles are concerned. Derived from OE *weorth* (worthy) + *scipe* (-ship, condition, office, profession) gave *weoth-scipe* to ME worship, a word peculiar to English.

zeal, ardour for a cause or, less often, for a person. From Gk *zeo* (boil), *zelos* through Lat and OF *zéle* to ME.

NOTE: the dipthong 'th' in Anglo-Saxon is called a 'thorn' and was represented in manuscripts by the sign 'þ'. Y or y were often used by printers as a makeshift so gradually the 'þ' died out and the word 'þe' for 'the' was written 'ye'. This however, should be pronounced 'the' not 'ye'. Phrases like 'ye olde inne' as a smart description of the local pub are rubbish.

PART II

Glossary of the Royal Arch Ritual

AL (Anno Lucis), the year of light which the ancients considered as 4000 BC ie the biblical date of the Creation. The Hebrew calendar dates the Creation as 3760 years before the Christian era. The RA dating is from the start of the Second Temple 570 BC, so that AD 1991 becomes *Anno Inventis* (or the year of discovery 2521.

annihilation, to reduce to nothing; to destroy completely. From Lat *annihilatus* the pp of *annihilare* — *ad* (to) + *nihil* (nothing).

arch, a bow-like curve, structure or object. In architecture, a structure supported at both ends and made of distinct pieces. The centre stone is usually called the arch- or keystone. The arch, as a means of building, was known some 400 years before the building of the Temple.

The masonic association between the arch and the rainbow should be noted as appearing in early rituals and biblically alluding to God's covenant with man. From the Lat *arcus* or *arquus* — (anything curved, a bow) to OF *arche*.

Ark, original meaning was a cover, coffin or chest, hence the chest used to hold the tablets of the Sacred Law in the Tabernacle. A derived meaning is a flat-bottomed boat and thus Noah's Ark (Genesis 6 vv 14-22) and Moses's cradle (Exodus 2 v 3). From AS *arc*, L *arca* (a chest). The French for 'ark' is *'arc'* and this has caused confusion in masonic literature with the 'arch' of Royal Arch.

atone-ment, the act of making expiation for some sin or crime. The Day of Atonement was the day on which the Israelites prayed to expiate their sins of the past year. A combination of AS *act* (at or to) and ME *at* with AS *an* (one or on) forming ME atone *ie* agree, appease, reconciliate.

beneficence, the habitual quality of bringing about or doing good, characterised by charity or kindness. From Lat *bene* (well) + *facere* (to do) forming *beneficientium*. Benevolence is synonym.

buckler, a shield, specially a small round shield designed to ward off blows. OF *bucler* (F *bouclier*) from Lat *buccula* (cheek-strap of a helmet, buckle).

catenarian, the curve shaped by a flexible, thin cord held suspended at both ends.

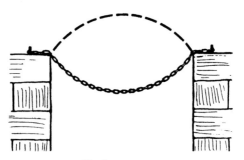

The Catenary Arch.

This curve is supposed to be the strongest architecturally of all curves. From Lat *catenarius* and *catena* (a chain).

censer, a vessel for burning incense. Used in churches *etc* as incense is a symbol of purity or pure thought. The word is a shortened form of the root essence which comes through OF from Lat *Incensum*, the pp of *incendere* (to burn) — incense presumably being a distillation.

chaos, yawning emptiness, the confusion said to have existed at the Creation. From F *chaos* and Gk *Chaos* (*chachaskein* to gape).

chapter, a branch of a society or a meeting place, usually of clergy. Monks meeting in an assembly, presided over by the head of their house, often had read passages from a sacred book *ie* a chapter. It is not known why Masons adopted the word for their meetings but it dates from very early days when, in the reign of Henry VI, 1445, they were forbidden to meet in chapters. From Lat through F *chapitre*, *capitulum*, a diminutive of *caput* (head).

conciliate, to win the regard of or to over-come the hostility of, or pacify. From L *concilium* (a council) from *con* (together) + *ciliare* (to call).

conclave, a secret council or meeting. Some inner workings in Masonry. The cardinals of the Roman Catholic church are locked in during the papal election. F *conclave* from Lat *conclave cum* (with) + *clavis* (a key). In Gk, the word from which *clavis* is derived is *klavis* (a key).

congregate, to bring together in a crowd. Lat *con* or *cum* (with or together) + *gregare* (to collect) derived from *gregis* (a flock).

consecrate, to devote or dedicate to sacred use. All masonic bodies have to be consecrated before allowed to act. Lat *con* or *cum* (together) + *secrare* (to be holy) produces *consecratus*.

constitute, to establish by proper authority. In masonry, normally this is by the issue of a warrant or charter. Lat *constitutus*, the pp of *constituere* from *con* (together) + *statuere* (cause to stand, put in place).

contiguous, touching or joining at the edge or boundary. Lat *contiguus* from *con* (together) + *tangere* (touch).

contrite-ition, broken in spirit because of the sense of penitence. F *contrit,* Lat *contritus* pp of *conterere, con* (together) with *terere* (to grind, to rub).

convocation, an assembly or council called together by an individual or an authority F *convoquer,* L *convocare* from *con* (together or with) + *vocare* (to call).

covenant, an agreement between two or more people, a compact, specially the Almighty's promises of blessing on the fulfilment of a condition or promise. The first covenant in Scripture was between

God and Abraham (Genesis 10). OF present p of *convenir*. Lat *convenire* from *con* (together) + *venire* (to come).

criterion, a standard by which to judge the correctness of a decision or a test. From Gk *kriterion* derived from *kritis* (a judge).

crow, there seems no reason why this shortened form of crow-bar should be used in the ritual. A crow-bar is a straight metal bar flattened or squared at one end to act as a lever. This is supposed to be like the beak of the bird, a crow. Crow is derived from AS *crawan*, its cry being AS *Crawe*.

Cyrus, was the founder of the Persian Empire and captured Babylon in 538 BC. He reigned from 559 BC until 529 BC when he was killed in battle and succeeded by his son Cambyses. The Edict of Cyrus which led to the rebuilding of the Temple at Jerusalem and the start of Judaism is fully described in the ritual. See also 2 Chronicles 36 v 22 and Ezra 1.

dispensation, in the ritual the word appears to mean God's dealing with man, particularly the divine relation to man at a certain period of time (as God's dealing with Abraham). The more normal meaning of the word is the act of distribution and now specially of administrative rights. An important further meaning in Masonry is that of a document authorizing the change in some rule *ie* the date of a meeting. Comes into English through OF *dispenser* and L *dispensare* or *dispendere,* both derived from *pendere* (to weigh).

disquisition, a formal inquiry or a systematic literary or verbal presentation of a subject. In the ritual it seems to mean the way in which the principles of the degree are presented. It is the same root as 'question'. From Lat *dis* (apart) + *quaerere* (to seek).

dome, the vaulted roof of a circular building. Gk *domos* (a house) through Lat and F.

double or doubled cube, is a solid bounded by six equal square faces (*hexahedron*) and having its angles all right angles. The altar in the ritual is based on that in Exodus 30 vv 1-2 and is an altar of incense. Only a small altar would be needed and verse 2 shows it was a double cube: 'A cubit shall be the length thereof,

The Pedestal in the form of a doubled cube.

and a cubit the breadth thereof: four square shall it be; and two cubits shall be the height thereof.' Cube is from F derived from Lat *cubim* and Gk *kubus*.

element-al, relating to a first principle or primary parts. The word has developed a specially scientific sense. From Lat *elementum* (beginning).

elucidate, to throw light on, to clear up, explain. From Lat *elucidatus* pp *elucidare, e* or *ex* (out) + *lucidus* (light).

enunciate, to pronounce clearly or by syllables, to disclose, make a formal announcement. From Lat *enuntiatus* pp of *enuntare*; *e* (out) + *nuntius* (announce). This root appears in Papal Nuncios who are the messengers or ambassadors of the Pope.

essence, that which constitutes the nature of something, a solution or extract. From F, through Lat *essentia* (being) from *esse* to be).

exalt-ation, the procedure of RA degree. The word means to raise up in position or rank. It also means the state of rejoicing as a result of being raised up. Early Masons would have been inspired by the extensive biblical use of the word: *eg* Psalm 89 v 19. 'I have exalted one chosen out of the people' and the feeling of joy that the Virgin Mary shows in the Magnificat (Luke 1 v 52) 'He has put down the mighty from their seats and exalted those of low degree.' Such quotations amply sustain the meaning of RA Masonry. From Lat (through F) *ex* (out) + *altus* (high).

excellent, having good qualities of a high standard. The title has been used since early days by Masons for the titles of certain degrees and high officials. The titles for the principles in RA Masonry certainly date from the first Chapter of the Premier Grand Lodge as it was called The Excellent and Royal Chapter; and its brethren were Most Excellent or Excellent Companions. It is not known whether the RA Masons of the other Grand Lodges entitled themselves similarly. There were a number of 'Excellent' degrees in the 18th century. The word comes through Rom languages from the Lat *excellere* — *ex* (out) + *celsus* (raised).

Exodus, the second book of the Old Testament describing the Israelites' departure from Egypt and their wanderings in the Wilderness of Sinai. The word has the general meaning of the departure or going away of a large body of people. From Gk (and L Lat) *ex* (out) + *hodos* (a way).

expound-er, to set forth the meaning of; to explain; or to interpret or those who do so. To ME *expounen* and OF *expondre* from Lat *exponens*, the present p of *exponere* (to put).

Ezra, (Hebrew — help) called Esdras in the Apocrypha. He was a pious and learned priest living in Babylon in the reign of Artazerxes. In 457 BC he received permission to go to Jerusalem with a company of Israelites. His great design was to effect a religious reform among the Palestinian Jews. The date of his death is not known. The authorship of the books of Chronicles, Ezra and Nehemiah — or parts of them — is attributed to him. It will be seen that he was not a contemporary of Zerubbabel.

fiducial, indicates confidence, trust. This is the meaning that can be accepted from the ritual aspect. The word however is now more or less archaic, except from the financial meaning of a trust or trusteeship. As descriptive of a masonic gesture, it must be accepted as being purely symbolical. From Lat *fiducialis*, from *fiducia* (trust), from *fidere* (to trust), *fides*, (faith).

gradation, a regular advancement up or down steps. The progress of a Mason through the various degrees and rites is an example of gradation. The word is usually in the plural. From Lat *graditionem*, from *gradus* (a step).

gravitate, to be moved by the force of gravity *ie* the accelerating tendency of bodies towards the centre of the earth or to any other heavenly body. From the Lat *gravitare* from *gravis* (heavy).

Haggai, (Hebrew — festive), a minor prophet who testified after the return of the Israelites to Jerusalem under Zerubbabel. Nothing is known about his history or parentage. It is also not known if he was in Zerubbabel's party, as his name is not listed. He started to urge the Israelites towards good behaviour and the completion of the Temple in the second year of the reign of Darius, probably 522/1 BC (See Ezra 5 v 1 and Haggai 1 v 1).

holden, an archaic use of the past tense of the verb 'to hold'. It is not known why those compiling the ritual retained it, except possibly because the word is close to the AS origin of the word *healdan* or *halden* (hold).

homage, to pay respect or reverence to. Under feudal laws, it was the formal acknowledgment of tenure by the tenant to the lord of the manor. Legal obligation for homage and the consequent feudal dues have died out but are retained in many parts of UK — notably the Channel Islands — as a ceremonial procedure. Homage is an OF word derived from the L Lat *homaticum* one of the many words stemming from *homo* (a man).

injunction, the act of requiring a person to do or to refrain from doing something. In modern English, almost entirely restricted to legal usage. In such cases an injunction is served by a writ or process. From Lat *in* (in) + *jungere (to join)*.

inkhorn, a holder for ink; so called because it was usually made of horn. The first mention of writing in the Bible is Exodus 17 v 14 when 'the Lord said unto Moses, Write this for a memorial in a book and rehearse it in the ears of Joshua', but there is no indication what writing implements were used. It is thought that writing was started by the very early Phoenicians but again no implements are known. It is known that the dark fluid from cuttlefish was used. An indication of early ink-making comes from the derivation of the word. Ink came into English from OF *enque*, F *encre*, L Lat *encaustum*. Purple ink used by the Roman Emperors comes from the Gk *enkaustos* (burnt in) shows that burning may have been the way ink was originally made.

Insignia, any form of badge used to mark the wearer's rank of office. The word

Obverse and reverse of the Royal Arch jewel.

includes regalia worn: and in the Royal Arch this is extensive and complicated. The word is the Lat plural of *insigne* (a mark of distinction) and is derived from *in* (on) + *signare* (to mark). The word possibly came into English through the AS *segnium*.

inspiration, to breathe into the lungs or inhale, hence symbolically the breathing in of a lofty thought, emotion or creative power, as shown in art, literature etc. From Lat *inspiro* — *in* (in) + *spirare* (to breathe) and OF *enspirer*.

intuitive, seen by the immediate understanding of the mind; seeing at once and clearly. From F through L Lat. The noun 'intuition' is from *intuitionem* from *intueri* — *in* (in) + *tueri* (to look).

irradiate, to shed light upon, to make bright or brilliant, to light up. Many masonic jewels have insignia irradiated by lines drawn outwards like the spokes of a bicycle wheel *ie* radii. In the RA, the jew-

els of the Chapter Principals are an irradiated crown, eye and VSL respectively.
From Lat *irradiatus* pp of *irradiare* — *in*
(in, into) + *radius* (ray).

janitor, the doorkeeper of a Royal Arch
Chapter. In early chapters, he was called
the 'Tiler' and it is likely that the term was
adopted to make a distinction. The word is
derived from Lat *janua* (a door), probably
derived in its turn from Janus, the Sun-
god, because the door lets in light.

Jehoiachin, (Hebrew — Whom God hath
appointed), he was the son of Jehoiakim,
the king of Judah who lost his kingdom
and was a vassal first of the Egyptians
and then of Nebuchadnezzar. When
Jehoiakim was killed, he was succeeded
by his son Jehoiachin, who was eighteen
years old (2 Kings 24 v 8) (but only eight
according to 2 Chronicles 36 v 9). both
books accuse him of doing evil in the
'sight of the Lord'. He only reigned for 3
months and ten days in Jerusalem before
being deposed by Nebuchadnezzar and

taken to Babylon together with all the men of Judah except for the very poorest who were left behind to till the land.

Joshua or Jeshua, (Hebrew — a saviour), Son of Jehzadek, high priest during the Babylonian captivity 536 BC. Jeshua was probably born in Babylon where his father had been taken captive when young (1 Chronicles 6 v 15). He went from Babylon in the first year of Cyrus's reign (538-529) with Zerubbabel, and took a leading part with him in the rebuilding of the Temple and the restoration of the Jewish nation. Joshua is a common Jewish name and men of that name appear frequently in biblical history and may cause confusion. Joshua, the son of Nun (Nehemiah 8 v 17) is quite a different person from the son of Jozadek, though mentioned in contemporary biblical literature.

keystone, the uppermost and last set stone in an arch. It locks the other stones together and completes it. As a result, the word is often used figuratively. The word archstone, often similarly used, is merely one of the stones in the arch and not the key. From the AS *caeg* (a key) + *stan* (stone).

lector, an archaic term for one who reads, formerly was normally applied to whoever was reading the Scriptures in a church or school. From L Lat *lector* (a reader) and *legere* (to read). The modern word is lecturer.

manifold, of great variety, numerous. Now its use is pretentious and stilted. From AS *manig* (many) + AS *feald* (many times or repetitious).

mediatorial, implies the process of acting as an intervening body between parties in order to calm tempers or reconcile differences. Now also to pacify or harmonize. From L. Lat *mediatus* the pp of *mediare* — to divide in the middle from *medium* (middle).

mitre, a headdress sometimes worn by priests of Christian religions. It is a tall, ornamental cap terminating in two peaks.

In spite of its use in some Royal Arch chapters by the Principal in the priestly office, the High Priest's headdress would not have been a mitre but a turban mounted on an encircling plate of gold on which was inscribed 'Holiness to the Lord'. From Gk *mitra*, probably coming into English through the F *mitre*.

monitorial, the adjective describing one who warns or admonishes. The modern meaning of one who listens in, particularly to radio activity, has no connection with the Royal Arch naturally, while the original meaning is becoming old-fashioned. From Lat *monitus* pp of *monere* (to advise, admonish or instruct).

Nebuchadnezzar, was the greatest and most powerful of the Babylonian kings. In the lifetime of his father, he defeated the Egyptians, recovered Syria, Phoenicia and Palestine, took Jerusalem (Daniel 1 v 1) and was on his way to Egypt when his father died and he succeeded him. Three years later there was a revolt in Palestine which Nebuchadnezzar suppressed, killing Jehoiakim the King and putting his son Jehoiachin on the throne. The latter proving seditious, Nebuchadnezzar took him to Babylon with many of the population. The new king, Zedekiah revolted some years later and Jerusalem was totally destroyed. During his reign, he rebuilt Babylon including the wonder of the world 'the hanging gardens'. After a period of mania, from which he recovered, he died in 561 BC having reigned forty three years.

Nehemiah, (Hebrew — consolation of the Lord), a Nehemiah accompanied Zerubbabel on his first journey from Babylon to Judah (Ezra 2 v 2 and Nehemiah 7 v 7) but there is no further information about him. The more important Nehemiah lived many years later and was cupbearer to King Artaxerxes about 445 BC. Jews returning from Palestine gave a deplorable account of the conditions there and Nehemiah got himself appointed governor of Judea. His great work was the rebuilding of the walls of Jerusalem, though in this he was hampered by the surrounding tribes. After some years, Nehemiah returned to Babylon but later went to Jerusalem once more and seems to have remained there until his death some years later. The ritual seems to have confused the two Nehemiahs attributing the works of the second to the period of the first. The second certainly was not a scribe but a high civil servant in the Babylonian Empire. Ezra and the first Nehemiah lived decades apart and would never have met.

noxious, causing or tending to cause injury to health or morals, pernicious. From Lat *noxius* (hurt, harm, injury) — *nocere* (to harm).

Omniscient. Omnipotent. Omnipresent, the three attributes of the Supreme Being *ie* infinite knowledge, unlimited power and present in every place at the same time. The words derive from the Lat prefix *omnes* (all or in all things) with Lat *scientia* (knowledge), the pp of *scire* (to know): Lat *potens* pp of *posse* (to be able) and Lat *praesentium* pp of *praeesse* (to be in a place).

parchment, sheep or other skins polished, possibly with pumice-stone, and used for writing. The Dead Sea scrolls, discovered this century, show that this form of writing material is of very early origin. Through F *parchemin* to Lat *pergamena* (pertaining to Pergamum), a city in Asia Minor where presumably it originated.

penitential, pertaining to a sense of one's own guilt and a desire to do better in future, being contrite, an admission of wrong-doing. Through OF from Lat *paenitentum* the present p of *paeniteri*, related to *punire* (to punish).

pickaxe, a shafted tool with a cross piece; one end having a point and the other a chisel-like end. Through ME *piken* from AS *pycan* to F *piquer* (to prick) + AS *eax* or *aex* (axe). The word is possibly related to pike, the weapon which is from AS *pic*.

platonic bodies, these solids are part of the furniture of a chapter. Plato is reputed to have considered the Tetrahedron as the symbol of the element fire; the Hexahedron (or Cube), as that of earth; the Octahedron as that of water; the Icosahedron as that of air; while he took the Dodecahedron as the symbol of the universe itself. They do not appear in all the rituals and the suggestion is that their inclusion is comparatively modern, that is dating from the revision after the Union. In any event, the connection with Masonry is obscure. The words describe the shape of the various solids and are a connection of the Gk

The Platonic Bodies

tetra (four triangular solids); *hexa* (six equal sides and thus a cube); *okto* (eight equal planes); *dodeka* (twelve equal planes; *eikosi* (twenty equal planes) + *hedra* (a seat or base). (See HC 249-251).

polity, the form or method or government of a state or a church. The word should not be confused with policy which is the plan of action resulting from the work of such a polity, or any form of administrative action. Both words are derived, through F from the Gk word *politeia* (polity). The root is Gk *polis* (city) which has many derivatives *eg* police, metropolis.

precept, an ordered rule of conduct, a command, an injunction respecting conduct, a maxim. Through OF (F *précepte*) from Lat *praeceptum*, pp of *praecipre* — *prae* (from) + *capere* (to take).

preconcerted, the past tense of the verb preconceive. To compose or arrange beforehand. From Lat *prae* (before) + *cum* (with) + *certare* (to decide).

predominant, superior to, able to prevail over others. Through F *prédominer* from Lat *praedominare* — *prae* (before) + *dominor* (dominant); the root being *domus* (a house) *ie* the ruler of a house.

preferment, advancement, promotion, usually of a clerical nature. Through OF *préferer* (to bring forward) from Lat *prae* (before) + *ferre* (to bring).

primordial, first in order of time, original, primitive. Through F from L Lat *primordiatis* from *primordium* (origin) and *primus* (first) + *ordiri* (to begin). The word may be considered as archaic, except in masonic usage.

principal, head, chief leader. The change of title from Master of a lodge to Principal was gradual in the RA and seems not to have been completed until the ritual revisions after the Union of 1813 and the following years. Through F from Lat *principalis* and *principe* (chief). The word 'principle' denoting a moral truth etc has a different Lat root *principium* (a beginning).

promulgate, to announce publicly, proclaim officially, make known to the public. When the ritual of the RA was revised, a temporary Chapter of Promulgation was formed (in 1835) to demonstrate the new system. From Lat *promulgatus*, pp of *promulgare* (to make known). The etymology is uncertain, possibly a corruption of *provulgare* — *pro* (for or in favour of) + *vulgus* (crowd).

prophetical, pertaining to divine inspiration, referring to the sayings of a religious leader. The Bible contains the writings of a number of major and minor prophets but there are mentions of many others of whose stature or genuineness, nothing is known. The term 'false prophet' occurs frequently. The word is derived from the Gk *prophetes* — *pro* (before) + *phemi* (speak).

propitiation, now virtually archaic. The act of being kindly disposed, gracious, attended by favourable circumstances, auspicious. There are many adequate synonyms *eg* reconciliation, expiation, giving satisfaction. Lat *propitiatus* pp of *propitiare* — *pro* (from) + *petere* (to fly). Possibly a term used in augury or soothsaying.

prototype, a primitive form, an original form, an example. F from the Gk *proto-tupon* — *protos* (first) + *typos* (type).

providence - ial, basically the result of the care exercised by the Supreme Being over the universe, hence provision, foresight, timely care, prudence. F from Lat *providentia* from *pro* (for, in favour of) + *videre* (to see).

revelation, the act or process of giving knowledge, specially communications by divine agency as the doctrines of the Bible, or the Bible itself. From OF through Lat *revelatus* the pp of *revelare* (to reveal) — *re* (back) + *velum* (a veil).

reverential, expressing profound respect, often mixed with awe. The noun is reverent and should not be confused with reverend which is the title normally used by clerygmen. Both words have a similar root coming from Lat through F — *re* (again) + *vereri* (to fear or reverence).

robe, a long, loose, flowing garment worn over other clothing. The robes worn by the Principals of a RA Chapter are traditional and also symbolical. It is known that they were worn in early years of the degree. They take their significance from biblical texts. 'And this is the offering which shall take of them (the Israelites for making the Tabernacle). And blue, and purple, and scarlet' (Ex 25 v 1 & 4) and 'Moreover thou shalt make the tabernacle with ten curtains of fine twined linen, and blue, and purple, and scarlet.' (Exodus 26 v 1). The surplices worn by the scribes and sojourners appear only to be from *c* 1782. They may be a development of the alb, a linen vestment worn originally in Gk and L days and worn by Christian priests from about the 3rd century. From the F *robe* or from AS, *reaf* (clothing).

sacerdotal, pertaining to the priesthood or to priests; priestly; attributing sacrificial power and supernatural or sacred character to priests. Lat *sacerdotalis* from *sacerdos -dotis* (priest) — *sacer* (holy) + *dare* (to give).

Sanctum Sanctorum, the Holy of Holies in the Jewish Temple. It was the innermost part within the veil and always in darkness. It contained only the Ark of the Covenant in which were the tablets of the Law inscribed with the Ten Commandments. There is biblical authority for the action of the High Priest's action described in the ritual (Leviticus 16, 23 to 26). Many similar words have the same Lat root of *sanctus* (holy).

Sanhedrin, the origin of this body can be traced to the seventy elders whom Moses was directed to associate himself with in the governing of the Israelites. But this body seems to have ceased to exist on the entry into Palestine. There is no evidence that a similar body was formed until much later than the period covered traditionally in the RA. The etymology of the names suggests a period subsequent to the Macedonian supremacy in Palestine 332 BC. Whenever it was formed, it seems to have had the form and composition suggested in the ritual, that is in a semi-circle of seventy wise men and with two scribes. No doubt Zerubbabel did have a council to advise him but to call it a Sanhedrin is an anachronism. The word is derived from the Gk *sanhedrion* — *syn* (with) + *hedra* (seat).

scribe, an ancient Jewish instructor in the Mosaic law, acting as a writer or interpreter. The original Hebrew word was *sopher*, plural *sopherum* (with the meaning of write, set in order or count). They were so-called because they wrote out the law, interpreted it and counted with scrupulous care every clause and letter it contained. In Solomon's time, they were little more than secretaries to important people but, over the centuries, they became more powerful and eventually their words were honoured almost above the Law itself. Their behaviour in the time of the New Testament often incurred the anger of Christ. The word scribe comes through F from the Lat *scriba* — *scribere* (to write).

scroll, a roll of parchment or paper, etc containing or intended to contain writing, also the writing it contained. The word was originally *scrowl* a diminutive of ME *scroue*, OF *escroue* (a strip) possibly from a German root *scrot*.

shovel, a flattened scoop with a handle for digging. From AS *scofen*, the pp of *scafan* (to dig) — *scofi*.

sojourn- er, to stay with temporarily or one who does so. The word appears a number of times in the Bible, a notable one being in Genesis 12 v 10 when 'Abram went down into Egypt to sojourn there' and Psalm 39 v 12 'I am a stranger with thee and a sojourner'. From about 1823 until 1886, there was the curious custom of the Principal Sojourner appointing his own assistants. The word is derived from Lat *sub* (under) + *diurnis* (daily) and OF *sojourner*.

staff (plural **staves**), a stick carried for some special purpose. As an aid to walking, climbing or as a wand of authority. The latter use appears to derive from the old custom of the treasurers of households carrying a staff as a symbol of their authority. In the Grand Lodge of England in 1741, the Grand Treasurer appeared 'with the staff'. From AS *staef*, (stick).

symmetry, due arrangement or balancing of the parts or elements of a whole with reference to one another; harmony. For example, the arrangements of parts on either side of a dividing line so that opposites are the same. From Gk *syn* (with) + *metron* (measure), through Lat *symmetria* and F *symétrie* to English.

tabernacle, a tent or booth or similar structure, specifically the portable sanctuary used by the Israelites to house their sacred symbols in their journey through the Wilderness of Sinai. F through *tabernaculum* Lat for a tent, a diminutive of *taberna* (shed or hut) *Mackey* has a full article on the Jewish Tabernacle.

tau, the 19th letter of the Gk alphabet and forms the 'tau cross'. In ancient times the letter was looked on as a symbol of life. The triple tau seems to be not earlier than the start of the 19th century. It is fully explained in the ritual but this geometrical interpretation has come since the complete joining of the T and the H and is probably not earlier than 1835. (See *Freemasons' Book of the Royal Arch*, B. E. Jones, 1981 reprint).

The Tau cross, T over H and the Triple Tau.

threshing-floor, an area for beating the stalks of ripe grain or seeds by means of a flail, thus separating the grain or seeds from the stalks or husks. One, the property of Araunah (Ornan) a Jebusite, was bought by King David as a site for the Temple (2 Samuel 24.16); the Jebusites being the original inhabitants of the Jerusalem area. From AS *threscan*. The same word etymologically is 'thrash' but now 'thresh' is used for beating corn and 'thrash' in other senses.

vault, an arched roof, also any subterranean compartment or cellar. Its supposed presence in the RA is an anachronism as a true vault was not known until the 12th century. From OF *volte* from *volt* (arched) and F *voûte*. These F words come from the Lat *volvere* (to roll).

vellum, fine parchment originally made from the skin of calves, or a manuscript written on it. The word has a complicated etymology starting with Gk *italos* (calf) and *etos* (year), then *vitulinus* (Lat for a calf) to F *velin* and ME *velim.*

vessel, a hollow receptacle, especially for holding liquids, as a jug, cup, barrel, etc hence a ship or craft of any kind. By custom the word usually denotes a large ship but etymoligically refers to anything hollow that floats or can contain a liquid. From Lat *vascellum*, a diminutive of *vas* (an earthen vessel) and OF *vaissel*, F *vaisseau.*

vouchsafe, to grant with condescension, to permit, to deign. Vouch is from Lat *vocare* (to call) and OF *voucher*, *vocher* + Lat *salvus* (whole or *uninjured* and OF *sauf*. The word is now unusual enough to be deemed archaic but will remain extant owing to its use in prayer books.

Zerubbabel, (Hebrew- Born in Babel ie Babylon), in the first year of the reign of Cyrus, Zerubbabel was living in Babylon and probably the recognized leader of the Israelite captives. When Cyrus issued his decree, Zerubbabel led a party to some 42,000 released captives back to Jerusalem. The party included Jeshua, the High Priest, a Nehemiah and possibly Haggai, the prophet, though he is not listed in Ezra 2. Zerubbabel, who also had the Chaldean name of Sheshbezzar, was named as Governor of Judea. The rebuilding of the Temple proceeded spasmodically, partly because of the opposition of local inhabitants and partly lack of enthusiasm. The returned captives concentrated on houses for themselves until exhorted by Haggai.

Josephus, in his *Antiquities of the Jews* refers to a return visit to Babylon by Zerubbabel but the Bible does not mention it. No more is known of him and presumably he remained in Jerusalem until his death.

The name should be pronounced Zerub — bábel and not as in English chapters Zerúbb — abel with the accent on the syllable 'rub' but there is no chance of rectifying so long established a mistake.

CHRONOLOGY
of the period covered by the
Royal Arch Degree

BC

608   King Jehoiakim, King of Judah.

605   Nebuchadnezzar, King of Babylon, captured Jerusalem and takes some Israelites to Babylon. (Nebuchadnezzar reigned 605-564 BC).

602   Revolt of Israelites against Babylon.

597   Nebuchadnezzar again captures Jerusalem, deposes Jehoiakim and appoints Jehoichin as king. He reigns for three months but is then replaced by Nebuchadnezzar by Zedikiah, as King of Judah.

588-6   Zedikiah's revolt ends with capture and destruction of Jerusalem. More Israelites taken to Babylon.

582	Further captives to Babylon; only poorest left.
536	Cyrus King of Persia (538-529) Edict for return of Jews. First party leaves under Zerubbabel includes Jeshua, the high priest, Nehemiah and possibly Haggai, the Prophet.
535	Rebuilding of the Temple starts.
529-21	Cambyses, King of Persia.
522	Rebuilding of Temple stopped by royal decrees.
520	Rebuilding resumes by decree of Darius (525-481). Work urged on by Prophet Haggai.
515	Temple dedicated. Condition and attitudes of Israelites start to decline.
458	Commission of Ezra as Governor of Judea. (By Artexerxes 465-425 BC.)
444-433	Commission of Nehemiah to Jerusalem. Walls rebuilt, morale restored.
428	Second commission of Nehemiah to Jerusalem.

Note: The Nehemiah who accompanied Zerubbabel to Jerusalem in 536 BC was a scribe. Nehemiah who was sent to Jerusalem nearly a hundred years later was a senior civil servant. The ritual hardly makes it clear which is intended. The gap between Zerubbabel and the two, Ezra and the second Nehemiah, would thus be about 100 years.

PART III
Some additional words, not in the ritual, which require some explanation

Acception, the full title of English masons is 'Free and Accepted or Speculative'. Notes on FREE and SPECULATIVE are given earlier. A reference to masons being accepted dates from about 1620. At this period the London Masons' Company had some sort of 'inner circle'. The Company was an operative one and it is suggested that the 'inner circle' was some form of speculative lodge. Those in this special body were 'accepted' into it. (See *The Records of the Hole Crafte and Fellowship of Masons* 1894 by Edward Condor Jr.) The actual word 'acception' appears in the Company's records in 1684 though the words 'to accept' appear earlier. Various forms of the word appear in masonic documents on a number of occasions during the next century. In 1722, a masonic pamphlet uses the phrase 'free and accepted' and it becomes officially recognized by being in the 1738

Book of Constitutions. The phrase is now used by all the British Grand Lodges and many of those in USA. See also FGC 88-91 and HC 53-4.

Bumper, originally a leather cup but later was used to describe any individual drinking mug. The origin of the word comes from its being a corruption of 'bombard' a medieval engine of war for throwing large stones. This would have had the shape of a squat mug. In due course, bumper was used for any glass or metal drinking vessel. In the Exp *Jachin and Boaz* 1762, the candidate is instructed 'to take a bumper' to drink with. Such drinking vessels were used in lodges for masonic FIRE and would be solid. French drinking customs of about 1740 show that their cups were called 'cannon', significant but possibly only a coincidence. There is no connection between the word 'bumper' and banging the glass down on the table at the end of masonic FIRE. In some lodges, a 'bumper toast' is called for as a special honour. Whether this means a drink from a full glass or is to urge the drinkers to empty their glasses is not clear. In any case, neither is practicable and, in these breathalyser days, desirable; besides being a misuse of an archaic English word. As the expression does not mean what it says, it might be wiser to use the word 'hearty' instead.

Unanimous, this word is often misused. A unanimous vote is one in which all present have voted the same way. If there are any abstentions, the vote is not unanimous. When, though no one votes against the motion, one or more persons present abstain, the motion is carried *nem con* (L *nemine contradicente*). Normally all present should vote in a ballot, even if the candidate is not known personally. This is a vote of confidence in the proposer and seconder, or in any lodge investigating committee. This does not apply in lodges etc where names are circulated to all brethren for approval before being placed on a summons. Balloting is then only a legal formality and abstentions are quite in order. Ballots should always be announced as 'in favour of the candidate' or, if there are too many black balls, 'not in favour of the candidate'. The word is derived from L *unus* (one)+*animus* (mind).

Toast, the expression 'to toast' dates back to the 16th century where it seems to have been the custom for a piece of toasted bread to have been put into the loving cup before this was circulated. The toast was eaten by the host when the cup was returned to him. FGC suggests that the practice continues in some English universities. There is nothing specifically masonic about the word.

Upstanding, a request to the brethren to 'be upstanding' to drink a toast is an absurdity; in any case, as all toasts are drunk standing in lodges, it is an unnecessary instruction. It is only in the Royal Navy, and a few other bodies with special traditions, that toasts may be drunk while sitting. The word 'upstanding' is obsolete and its original meaning referred to a person's character, not his posture. It is therefore not the opposite of 'sitting-down'. If whoever is giving the toast feel it essential to give orders on the subject, it is suggested that he invite the brethren 'to stand and drink etc'.

The letter G, this is the 'Sacred Symbol' in the centre of the building referred to in the Second Degree. In the early 1700s it was usually drawn or represented by a templet in the middle of the floor of the lodge. It appears to be first mentioned in the exposure MD 1730:

Q. What does that G denote?

A. Geometry or the Fifth Science.

Geometry was for many years almost a synonym for Freemasonry with the Fellowcraft often being referred to as a G-letter man and Masons as a class called Geometer. But it also had a spiritual significance as the same exposure shows:

Q. What does the G denote?

A. One that is greater than you.

Q. Who is greater than I, that am a Free
   and Accepted Mason, the Master of
   a Lodge?

A. The Great Architect and Contriver of the Universe, or He that was taken up to the Top of the Pinnacle of the Holy Temple.

The accepted view is that the Supreme Being and Geometry have much in common; with Freemasonry and Geometry equally connected. The former appears always to have been in the minds of learned writers from as early as the time of Plato who said 'That God is a Geometer' and Milton in *Paradise Lost*:

Then stayed the fervid wheels, and in his hand

He took the golden compasses, prepared

In God's eternal store, to circumscribe

This Universe, and all created things,

One foot he centred, and the other turned

Round though the vast profundity obscure,

And said, 'Thus far extend, thus far the bounds,

This be they just circumference, O World!

The principle Characters in the RA Ritual. From the short biographies already given in the RA glossary, it is clear that Biblical history and the ritual do not agree. This is immaterial masonically as the degree is traditional. However, it seems worth recording the correct history for the record and for interest.

The final exile of the Jews to Babylon from Jerusalem was in 609 BC though many had been taken before. The first group to be repatriated under the leadership of Zerubbabel was in 538 BC. There were some 42,000 in this party. It included Joshua (or Jeshua) the High Priest, the son of Jehozadek, and one Nehemiah whose position was not described but he seems to have been a scribe. The prophet Haggai is not mentioned as being in this party in the Book of Ezra but Josephus, in the *Antituities of the Jews* names him as being with it. This seems likely as, in 520 BC, he was exhorting the returned exiles to complete the rebuilding of the Temple.

There is now another gap of about sixty years until 457 BC when a party of about

1,700 more Jews returned from Babylon
to Jerusalem. They were led by the priest,
Ezra who was also named as a scribe. He
was appointed governor of Judea but his
main task was to re-establish Jewish law
and morale generally. He was not wholly
successful as Jews returning to Babylon
reported, though this, according to Josephus, was after Ezra's death. The result of
the reports was that a Jew named
Nehemiah, who was a high civil servant
(cup-bearer to the King of Babylon)
obtained permission to go to Jerusalem as
Governor of Judea in 444 BC. He was
successful and the position improved.
Nehemiah returned to Babylon in
433 BC. He went once more to Jerusalem
as Governor in 428 BC where he seems to
have died. From the above, we can
deduce:

1. Haggai probably went to Jerusalem
   with Zerubbabel.
2. There were two Nehemiahs, one
   unimportant who probably was in
   the Zerubbabel party and many have
   been a scribe; and one, a very impor-

tant man who lived at least seventy years later and who was not a scribe.

3. Ezra and the second Nehemiah were nearly two generations later than the Zerubbabel party. In addition, they may never have met as Ezra died before Nehemiah went to Jerusalem.

The only reference in the ritual is in the Historical Lecture. 'The two Scribes represent Ezra and Nehemiah, Lectors and expounders of the Sacred Laws and attendants on the Grand Sanhedrin (which does not seem to have existed).'

(See *Whose Names they Bear* a pamphlet by Canon R. Tydeman and *Ezra the Scribe*, the Batham RA Lecture for 1985 by B. J. Bell — both will be found in most masonic libraries.)

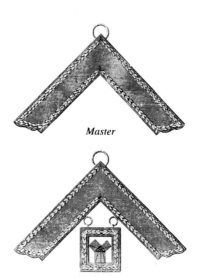

Master

Past Master

Senior Warden

Junior Warden

Chaplain

Treasurer

Secretary

Director of Ceremonies